# THE STORYBOOK OF *SCIENCE*

# THE STORYBOOK

ILLUSTRATED BY JEANNE BENDICK

# OF SCIENCE

## BY EARL SCHENCK MIERS

### RAND McNALLY & COMPANY
CHICAGO · NEW YORK · SAN FRANCISCO

# CONTENTS

# 1. ELECTRICITY: A Mystery
## It Took 2,500 Years to Solve

WHEN Bill awakened, the world outside his window was hidden by swirling snowflakes. The snow-laden branches on the trees made odd popping noises. In a strange way, Bill felt uneasy. He listened for the rattle of the train that carried his father to the city. It was time too for the clatter of the milkman's truck. But Bill heard none of the sounds normal to a new day. The boy switched on his bedside radio and a newscaster said:

"The storm that has raged all night is expected to continue all day. Many power lines, heavily laden with snow, have blown down. Repair crews are working around the clock to restore electricity in these areas. Now for a list of school closings—

"All schools in Grandview are closed," the announcer continued. "Also schools in—"

The radio went dead. In exasperation, Bill turned up the volume. Nothing happened. He looked into the set. All the tubes were dark. Then, from downstairs, he heard Mother speaking excitedly to Father:

"The lights have gone off!"

"Our power line must have broken," Father said.

"Oh, no!" Mother answered with a moan. "That means we're without electricity. Our oil furnace and refrigerator have stopped, and I can't use the vacuum cleaner or washer—"

*Without electricity!* With that phrase echoing in his ears, Bill ducked under his blankets and decided that he would stay where he was, snug and warm, until the power line was fixed. "Gee," Bill thought, "just one old snow storm cutting off the electricity and the whole world turns topsy-turvy!" Or a wind storm or flood or hurricane could do the same thing. And then—

Bill made a game of thinking of the changes that came into his world the instant there was no electricity.

No radio, no television, no streetcars running, no electric trains, perhaps no beacons to guide airplanes and ships to safety—a mess.

No machines running in factories—even the electric drill and saw in Dad's workshop became worthless. And at night, when he wanted to read, there would be no lights.

Why, Bill thought, he might as well be Abe Lincoln growing up in a cabin on the Indiana frontier!

### The Amber Rod

Luckily the living room could be shut off from the remainder of the house, and with logs burning cheerily in the fireplace, the family could keep warm until the power line was repaired.

THE PAPER JUMPED UP OFF THE TABLE

"I'll be glad when there's electricity in this room again," Bill said.

"But there is," Dad answered. "We can't use it, but it's here nonetheless." When Bill looked unbelieving, Father said: "I'll prove it."

Dad sent Bill for a piece of wool cloth and a rubber comb. He told Bill to rub the comb with the wool. Then he placed a bit of paper on the coffee table and directed the boy to hold the comb near it.

"Why, the paper jumps up to the comb," Bill said.

Dad nodded, explaining that what Bill had just discovered had made a Greek philosopher named Thales famous. Thales had what Dad called an itchy foot, for he traveled constantly. He also had an itchy mind, for he was curious about everything—the wind, the stars, the tides. In time Thales learned how to astonish his friends by telling them right to the day when to expect an eclipse of the sun or moon. Among people who believed that a dragon lived in the sky and tried to swallow the sun or moon whenever the fancy struck him, Thales seemed a wonder—the philosopher who could outthink a dragon!

About 600 years before the birth of Christ, this wise Greek made another startling discovery. Thales found that if he briskly rubbed an amber rod with a cloth, small pieces of feather or the pith of plants would cling to the amber. In time these objects dropped off, so Thales gave his rod another hard rub and back they came.

"What is amber?" Bill asked.

Father pointed to the yellow mouthpiece of his pipe stem. "That's amber," he said. "Millions of years ago, probably in Northern Europe, a great upheaval of the earth's surface buried many pine trees under ground and under water. The sap in those trees gradually hardened into this substance which we call amber and the Greeks called *elektron*."

THALES, WITH AMBER ROD AND FEATHERS

## Untangling the Mystery

Thales couldn't explain why the pieces of feather or pith clung to the amber rod. Almost 700 years later a Roman, named Pliny the Younger, found that a lodestone (or magnet) would attract metals in the same way, but he still couldn't tell anybody why. Then in the time of Queen Elizabeth, which is jumping ahead 1,400 years, a physician named William Gilbert added sulfur, glass, and resin to the list of materials that, when rubbed with a cloth, acted much like the amber rod Thales had used. Dr. Gilbert wrote a book about his experiments, calling the science he helped to invent *electricity*. An object when rubbed, said these early experimenters, gave off an electric *charge*.

What all these men were discovering is known as *static electricity*, the same kind of electricity that drew the paper to the rubber comb. It is this kind of electricity that gives you a shock when, on a cold day, you walk across a carpet and then touch another person or a metal doorknob. It took almost two hundred years more to learn that there are two kinds of electricity as different as day from night. One kind we call *positive* and the other *negative* and each has set notions of what constitutes polite behavior.

Bring one negative charge in contact with another negative charge and each will try to get as far from the other as possible. Two positive charges will behave the same way. But let a negative charge meet a positive charge and they form a happy partnership.

"If you watch the garage mechanic when he changes the battery on our car next time," Dad said, "you will see that one side is marked plus (+) for the positive charge, and the other side is marked minus (—) for the negative charge. What the man from the service station

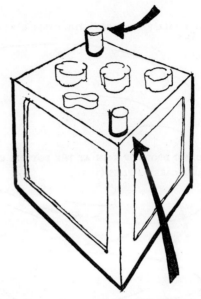

ONE SIDE OF A BATTERY IS MARKED PLUS (+) ONE SIDE IS MARKED MINUS (—)

can't always tell you is that the man who first suggested using + and — for the two kinds of electricity was wise old Benjamin Franklin. It was the notion of this great American that objects contained a strange fluid. Franklin believed, moreover, that an object could have too much or too little of this fluid, thus accounting for the two kinds of electricity. In this case Franklin was dead wrong, but in science, as long as you keep honestly trying to learn, a mistake now and then is of little importance."

## But Ben Had a Good Idea, Too

One thing Ben Franklin was not mistaken about was the lightning rod. When Franklin puzzled over inventing such a rod, more than two hundred years ago, nobody knew much about clouds. For example, nobody knew that the big drops of rain, which always settle at the bottom of a cloud, for some mysterious reason carry a plus charge of electricity, or that the smaller drops of rain in the upper part of the

THE SMALL RAINDROPS IN THE UPPER PART OF A CLOUD CARRY A MINUS CHARGE

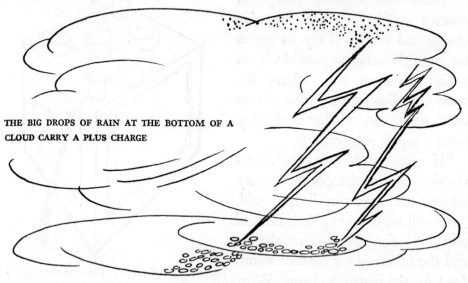

THE BIG DROPS OF RAIN AT THE BOTTOM OF A
CLOUD CARRY A PLUS CHARGE

IF AIR DOES NOT FLOW BETWEEN TO KEEP THEM APART, WE GET LIGHTNING

cloud carry a minus charge. As long as there is enough air flowing between these big and little raindrops nothing happens, but let the air fail to hold those fellows apart and—wham!—you get a walloping spark. About nine out of ten of these sparks of lightning jump from one cloud to another, but Number Ten streaks toward the earth looking for a tree or rooftop.

Franklin had a good hunch about streak Number Ten. That streak, he believed, was electricity, and he was willing to risk his neck to prove it. With a pair of bifocal glasses sliding down his nose—he also invented the glasses—Franklin crossed two sticks and stretched a large handkerchief over them. A mighty fine kite, he thought—light and strong—and on the next stormy day he intended to put his kite aloft. He planned to fly it with a cotton string which, when wet, invited electricity to run along it. At the end of the string he would hang a metal key. Then, since silk thread and electricity didn't seem to mix socially, he would give himself a length of silk thread to hold so that (he hoped) his body would be protected from the bolt of lightning.

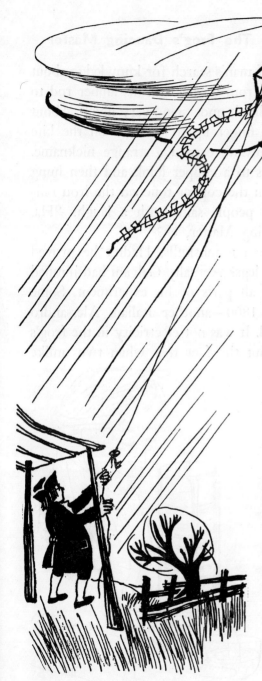

BENJAMIN FRANKLIN AND HIS KITE

At last a day arrived with dark clouds overhead and growling thunder and pelting rain. Franklin sent up his kite. He watched it dip and swerve in the wind, and then—bright and sharp—lightning leaped from a cloud. "Well," Ben must have thought with a gulp, "do I or don't I?" And his strong will answered: "You do!" He placed his finger near the key. A spark shot out.

So there was proof that lightning was electricity. Later, by giving lightning a metal rod (like Franklin's key), rather than a rooftop to strike, a wire from the rod carried the electricity into the ground without damaging the building. So Franklin's experiment demonstrated that lightning could be brought under control, and that electricity could be carried from one point to another.

### The Frog's Dancing Master

It had taken about 2,300 years of man's search for knowledge about electricity, Father estimated, to get from Thales and his amber rod to Franklin and his kite, and man still didn't understand very much. About forty years after Franklin held his finger up to the key on the kite string an Italian scientist, Luigi Galvani, earned a strange nickname. Galvani attached a pair of frog legs to a copper hook and then hung the hook over an iron railing. When the copper touched the iron railing, the legs twitched wildly and people said, with a laugh: "Ha, Galvani—so you're a Frog's Dancing Master, eh?"

But Galvani just scowled at such numbskulls. Hadn't he proved that there was electricity in a frog's legs? Actually Galvani had jumped at a conclusion without examining all parts of his experiment. Some fourteen years later—in the year 1800—another Italian, Alessandro Volta, saw what Galvani had missed. It was not electricity in the frog's legs that caused them to twitch, but the fact that when two unlike metals, such as copper and iron, are brought together, an electric current results.

"Volta, being a scientist with an inquiring mind," Father said, "had to do something with his discovery. And that something, as it turned out, was to prove that when a plate of copper is put in contact with a plate of zinc, the zinc produces (—) electricity and the copper (+) electricity."

Volta carried his experiment to the next logical step. He connected his positive (+) plate to his negative (—) plate with a

VOLTA'S BATTERY

wire and then watched what happened when he touched one of the plates with a fabric or paper dampened in a salt solution. An electric current passed between the two plates! So Volta had learned how to build a battery—it is called a *voltaic cell*—and man possessed his first practical source of electric current!

## But What **Is** Electricity?

"So far we've talked only about the way electricity acts," Bill complained. "We haven't said what electricity is. I know a battery starts our car and a lightning rod protects our house. Why?"

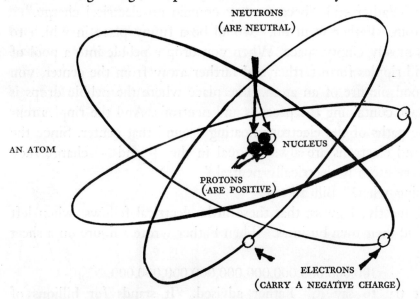

NEUTRONS
(ARE NEUTRAL)

AN ATOM

NUCLEUS

PROTONS
(ARE POSITIVE)

ELECTRONS
(CARRY A NEGATIVE CHARGE)

Father picked up a stick by the fireplace. "What you can't see," he said, "is that this stick, which looks so solid, is composed of bits of matter known as *atoms*. Everything is. That glass vase there, the rug on the floor, the steel frame of the lamp, the andirons on which the logs are burning are all composed of atoms. To measure across an atom would require a ruler with every inch divided into one hundred million parts."

Bill said: "There can't be anything smaller than that."

But Father insisted that there was—the parts of the atom itself. "In the center, or *nucleus*, of the atom," he explained, "are the *neutrons* and *protons*. And as far as they can get from the center are another group of particles called *electrons*."

Bill began to suspect what was coming: somewhere in the atom would be a place for Ben Franklin's + and — signs. And he was right, for Father said that the protons carry a positive or + charge of electricity and those standoffish particles that don't want to associate with other particles—the electrons—carry a negative or — charge. "The neutrons take nobody's side; they are neutral, as you can guess from the name," Father said, "because they contain no electrical charge."

"An atom," Father went on, "would be a funny place in which to live. It is mostly empty space. When you drop a pebble into a pool of water, and ripples form farther and farther away from the center, you have a good picture of an atom. The place where the pebble drops is the nucleus, containing the protons and neutrons. And the ripples represent the paths of the electrons floating around that center. Since the protons and electrons are always equal in the + and — charge they carry, every atom is electrically neutral."

"Meaning what?" Bill asked.

"Well, mostly, I guess, that these little electrical fellows, when left alone, mind their own business." Then Father wrote a figure on a sheet of paper:

300,000,000,000,000,000,000,000,000,000.

"Don't try to say it," Father advised. "It stands for billions of billions of billions. If you wanted to weigh up an ounce of electrons, neutrons, and protons, you'd need a figure that would have that many zeros."

"But if everything in the world is made up of atoms," Bill exclaimed, "then everything in the world must contain electricity!"

Father nodded. Right there, Bill had unlocked the main secret of electricity.

## Riddles Within a Riddle

What had happened when Bill rubbed the wool over the comb to pick up the bit of paper? Some of the electrons on the wool had rubbed off on the comb. Thus the balance in the atoms had been disturbed, and one substance had become *plus-charged* and the other *negative-charged*. Or, in an electrical sense, both had been ready for action.

"But," Father said, "there are riddles within this riddle. In some materials, such as metal, charges spread easily and are called *conductors* of electricity. In other materials, such as hard rubber or glass, the charges stay in place, and these materials are called *insulators*."

"Then a conductor is like the cotton string on Franklin's kite," Bill said, "or the wire that comes down from a lightning rod, or the plates in Volta's battery. Right?"

"Right. And an insulator," Father said, "is the silk thread Franklin held, or the air in a cloud that separates the big raindrops from the small ones, or the glass spools a power line is strung on."

"So it's the atom that makes it all work," Bill said in a rush. "And we can build dynamos—"

"Stop right there," Father cut in. "Do you remember what I told you about the Roman named Pliny the Younger?"

"Wasn't it that he understood that a lodestone, or magnet, would attract metals?" Bill asked.

"Yes, but Pliny the Younger had no idea that a relationship existed between electricity and magnetism. It was about 1,700 years later than his time—about 1819—that a professor in Denmark proved that electricity and magnetism were strangely related."

The professor's name was Hans Christian Oersted and he lived in Copenhagen. He knew about Volta's battery and he also knew that in England Michael Faraday had discovered that every magnet has both a north pole and a south pole. Like the + and — charges of electricity, two north poles or two south poles draw away from each other, but a north pole and south pole draw together. One day Oersted was about to disconnect a wire from a battery when an idea struck him. Nearby was a compass. "Just let's see," Oersted said, and he brought the wire close to the compass.

The unexpected happened. Instead of moving toward the wire, or away from the wire, the compass needle turned east. Oersted probably scratched his head and thought: "Suppose I change the wire on the poles of the battery so that the current runs in the opposite direction?" Again he held the wire above the compass—and the needle swung to the west!

Oersted had to believe what his eyes saw. "Let us imagine," Father said, "that, as you sometimes do in school, Oersted had to write an outline of what he had discovered." The outline might have read something like this:

### WHAT I, HERR PROFESSOR OERSTED, HAVE FOUND, TO MY SURPRISE

1. Electric current will move a compass needle, which is a magnet.
   A. But the needle moves *across* the current instead of toward and away from it.
   B. If there is no electric charge the magnet does not move.
2. Therefore, every conductor of electricity must be a magnet as long as the current flows through that conductor.
   A. We can call the force thus created a *magnetic field*.
   B. And the size of the magnetic field must depend upon the strength of the electric current that produced it.

### Others Get Into the Act

"On both sides of the Atlantic Ocean, other scientists began working on the principles Oersted had uncovered.

"In England, there was a shoemaker named William Sturgeon. He was an enthusiastic experimenter in electricity. Using the principles

ELECTRICITY CAN
MOVE A COMPASS
NEEDLE, BUT THE NEE-
DLE WILL SWING AT
RIGHT ANGLES TO THE
FLOW OF CURRENT

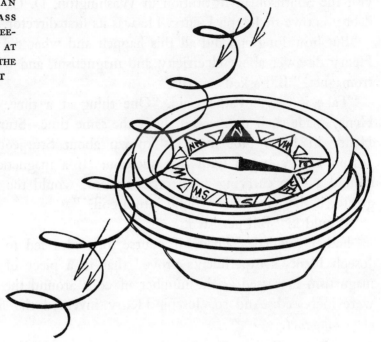

Oersted had uncovered, Sturgeon invented the first *electromagnet*. There are two kinds of electromagnets now in use, but that discovery was not made until later. The one we're interested in right now is the one Sturgeon invented—the kind that is used to lift things. Sturgeon's magnet was rather feeble and could lift only ten times its own weight.

"In the United States, Joseph Henry puzzled over the possibilities in what the Danish professor and the English shoemaker had demonstrated."

"Who was Joseph Henry?" Bill asked.

Father chuckled. "It was just luck, in a way, that Joseph Henry became a great scientist. He wasn't much of a student, and he had planned to be an actor. But one day, when he was ill, he passed the time reading a book about astronomy and chemistry. After that there was only one field of activity that interested Henry, and next time you visit the Smithsonian Institution in Washington, D. C., remember the debt you owe to Joseph Henry. He was its first director."

"But how long ago did all this happen and what did Sturgeon and Henry discover about electricity and magnetism, and what is an electromagnet?" Bill asked eagerly.

"Take it easy," Father said. "One thing at a time. Sturgeon and Henry made their discoveries about the same time—Sturgeon in 1825, Henry in 1826. Not much is known about Sturgeon's work, but Joseph Henry began with this question: 'If a magnetic field existed around a wire carrying an electric current, would the force become greater if the wire were wound into a coil?'"

"Would it?" Bill persisted.

Father nodded. "Then, of course, one idea led to another until Joseph Henry's experiments proved that in a piece of soft iron the magnetism increased as the number of coils around the piece of iron were increased. And so, Joseph Henry invented the first successful *electromagnet*.

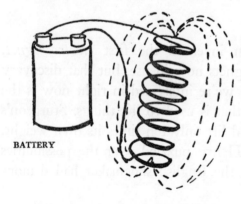

BATTERY

WHEN THE NUMBER OF COILS IS IN-CREASED, THE MAGNETIC FORCE BECOMES GREATER

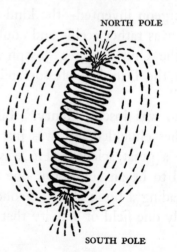

MAGNETISM SURROUNDS THE COIL WHEN CURRENT IS FLOWING

NORTH POLE

SOUTH POLE

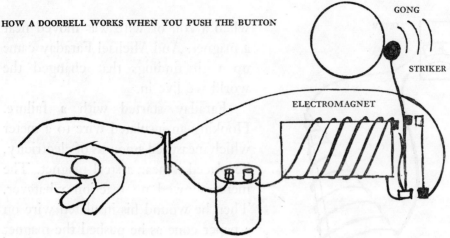

HOW A DOORBELL WORKS WHEN YOU PUSH THE BUTTON

GONG

STRIKER

ELECTROMAGNET

1. YOU COMPLETE THE CIRCUIT BE-
TWEEN THE BATTERY AND THE COILS

2. THE ELECTROMAGNET RELEASES THE
SPRING, AND THE STRIKER HITS THE GONG

"All such a device really amounts to," Father went on, to answer the last of Bill's questions, "is a number of coils of wire that act like a magnet when current is passed through them. Near one end an electromagnet has a north pole and near the other end a south pole. When there is no current, the coil or coils go back to being wire instead of an electromagnet."

Father laughed. "That was a lucky thing, too. When you push the button on a doorbell, completing the *circuit* between the battery and the coils, electromagnetism releases the spring that makes the striker hit the gong. When the button is released, the circuit is broken and without current the electromagnets go back to being coils of idle wire. A telephone rings the same way. It would require a big book to list all the uses we have for electromagnets, and today we can build electromagnets so strong that they can lift tons of steel or iron."

## Clever Michael Faraday

Around 1830, a few years after Joseph Henry invented the electromagnet, the Englishman who had discovered the north and south poles on magnets put his mind to work on the problem of what happened

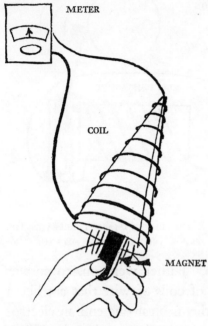

METER

COIL

MAGNET

MOVING THE MAGNET PRODUCED A
CURRENT IN THE COIL

when a coil of wire was moved near a magnet. And Michael Faraday came up with findings that changed the world we live in.

Faraday started with a failure. Hooking an insulated wire to a meter which measured amounts of electricity, he placed it near a steel magnet. The meter showed no reaction whatever. Then he wound his insulated wire on a paper cone as he pushed the magnet into the coil—and, like magic, the needle on the meter flipped. Without a battery, in that brief instant, Faraday had caused—or *induced*—a current of electricity in the wire! Faraday pulled his magnet out of the wire and the needle on the meter flipped again!

Now what in thunder did that mean?

In time Faraday saw the answer. When the magnet was in motion—and *only* when the magnet was in motion—it produced a current. The trick was that the magnet had to cut across the wire, creating the force. So clever Michael Faraday asked another question: "If a magnet were kept moving in and out of a coil (or revolving within a coil), what then?"

It was the question Faraday asked—and answered—that made it possible, some thirty years later, to build an *electric generator*, the forerunner of the great generating dynamos that today supply electricity to the homes of America. Some generators, like those at Hoover Dam on the Colorado River, can produce enough electric power to meet the needs of millions of people.

Faraday also proved that by placing a coil within two poles of a magnet, between which a current was passing, the coil would revolve.

"Think of that coil," Father said, "as mounted on a rod. Then assume that the coil and rod are set on an axle between the poles of a magnet. Then let's wind the wire on our coil so that when the current from a battery passes through it, one end will be an N-pole and the other an S-pole. Now if I turn the coil within the magnet or compass so that its S-pole is opposite the magnet's S-pole, the magnet will push it away, just as the magnet's N-pole will draw the coil's S-pole toward it."

"The old story of poles attracting or shunning each other," Bill said.

Father nodded. "When those opposite poles are in the position of natural attraction, everything should stop. But between the two ends of wire on our coil, I'm going to place a pair of brushes. These brushes are nothing like a hair brush. They're just small strips of copper used to make contact. I'll fix the brushes to slide over automatically, making the current reverse itself. Now our coil has to keep spinning so each

A SIMPLE ELECTRIC MOTOR

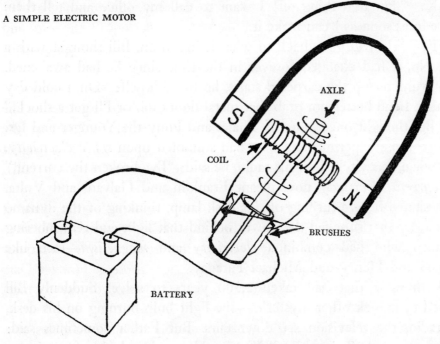

CURRENT FROM THE BATTERY FLOWS THROUGH THE COIL

end can find its new natural mate on the magnet. In its simplest form, do you know what I have?"

Bill looked puzzled and then annoyed because he thought he should know the answer. Finally he grumbled: "What?"

"An electric motor," Father said. "And again we should all say thanks—this time to Michael Faraday."

## And More Wonders to Come

Bill had been so fascinated by the conversation that he'd forgotten all about the broken power line. But all at once, as proof that it had been repaired, the lights flashed on. In the cellar the motor on the oil burner started with a hum and in the kitchen a little click sounded as the refrigerator started up. Then Bill almost jumped a foot, forgetting that he had turned up the full volume on his radio. Father said, rather crossly: "Shut that thing off! I want to call my office and tell them I'll be in as soon as I can make it."

His world had gone back to what it had been, Bill thought with a grin. No, it had changed forever in the time since he had awakened. Now, running up the carpeted stairs, he told himself: "On a cold day like this, I had better not grab that metal doorknob or I'll get a shock." And Bill thought once more of Thales and Pliny the Younger and Dr. Gilbert, those experimenters who had stumbled upon *static electricity*. And when he switched off his radio, he said: "I've broken the current," and *current electricity* now meant Franklin and Galvani and Volta. He hesitated before turning off his desk lamp, thinking of the dynamo miles away that supplied the power behind that light and remembering the men who had combined *electricity* and *magnetism*—men like Oersted and Henry and Michael Faraday.

A mystery that had taken 2,500 years to solve! Suddenly Bill wanted to unlock other mysteries—the light bulb burning on his desk, the radio, the television set downstairs. But Father sometimes said: "Rome wasn't built in a day." You could say that double for science.

## 2. ELECTRONICS: The Miracle
## Behind Radio and Television

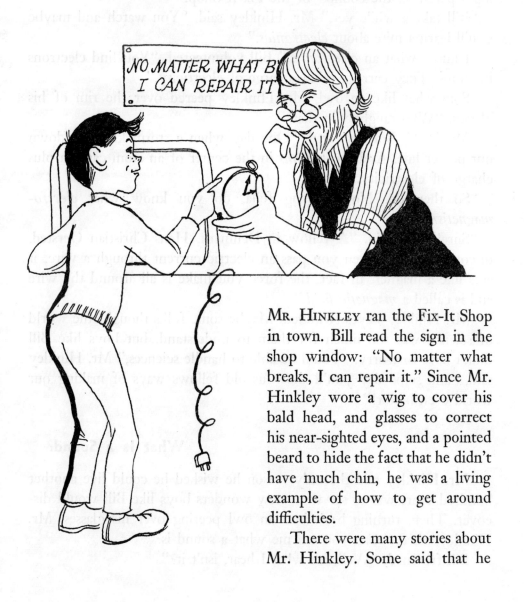

NO MATTER WHAT B
I CAN REPAIR IT

MR. HINKLEY ran the Fix-It Shop in town. Bill read the sign in the shop window: "No matter what breaks, I can repair it." Since Mr. Hinkley wore a wig to cover his bald head, and glasses to correct his near-sighted eyes, and a pointed beard to hide the fact that he didn't have much chin, he was a living example of how to get around difficulties.

There were many stories about Mr. Hinkley. Some said that he was a retired college teacher. Some said that he was an inventor and the richest man in town. But to Bill Mr. Hinkley was a trusted friend and the important things about him were his kindness and patience.

"When will you have our television set working?" Bill asked, clearing a perch on the counter of the Fix-It Shop.

"It'll take a while yet," Mr. Hinkley said. "You watch and maybe you'll learn a mite about *electronics*."

"I know what an *electron* is," Bill volunteered. "You find electrons in atoms. They carry a minus charge of electricity."

Somewhat like an owl, Mr. Hinkley peered over the rim of his glasses. "Who taught you that?"

"My Dad," Bill answered. "One day when a storm knocked down our power line. And the *protons* in the center of an atom carry a plus charge of electricity."

"So they do. Now, young fella, do you know what *electromagnetism* is?"

"Sure!" Bill said. "A fellow in Denmark, Hans Christian Oersted, discovered that. When you pass an electric current through a wire, it acts like a magnet. In fact, the force you make is all around the wire and is called a *magnetic field*."

Mr. Hinkley's eyes twinkled. Maybe some folks thought the world of science was too much for them to understand, but boys like Bill didn't have to worry. "You'll be able to handle sciences," Mr. Hinkley said, "and some day you'll show us old fellows ways of making our world even better!"

### What Is a Sound?

Mr. Hinkley said the only reason he wished he could live another hundred years was to see what new wonders boys like Bill would discover. Then, turning back into an owl peering over his glasses, Mr. Hinkley asked: "Can you tell me what a sound is?"

Bill frowned. "Well, it's what I hear, isn't it?"

"But what do you hear?" Mr. Hinkley asked. He took the alarm clock from the shelf over his workbench and asked Bill if he could hear it ticking. The boy nodded. Next Mr. Hinkley turned the clock face up on the workbench. The ticking grew louder.

"Hold your finger gently against the clock," Mr. Hinkley suggested. "What do you feel?"

"A series of little quivers," Bill answered.

"Or vibrations," Mr. Hinkley said. "When the clock is placed on the table, it has a larger surface on which to vibrate. The clock sounds louder because it makes more vibrations."

And what happens to those vibrations? "They travel through the air," Mr. Hinkley said, "and go into your ear. Here sensitive nerves carry the vibrations up to your brain. The brain changes the vibrations back into sounds that you recognize.

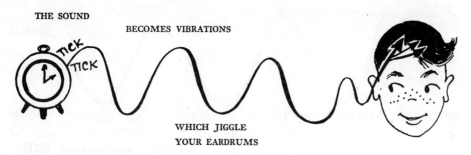

THE SOUND

BECOMES VIBRATIONS

WHICH JIGGLE
YOUR EARDRUMS

AND ARE CARRIED BY
NERVES TO YOUR BRAIN

"What I want you to remember," Mr. Hinkley said, "is that the sound becomes vibrations and the vibrations are turned back into sound. The secret of radio and television is that both sound and light can be changed into electricity and sent through the air before they are changed back into sound and light again.

"In one way," Mr. Hinkley added, "it might help to think of a midget cooped up inside the clock. Each time the clock ticks the midget swings a hammer. He hits the air and breaks it into particles. Of course the louder the sound, the harder he hits the air. So a sound is like a hammer blow. It is a force that moves the air.

"Yet how does sound move?" Mr. Hinkley asked. "It moves like a bouncing ball. And if you could draw a picture of the path made by a bouncing ball, your picture would also look like the top of a wave, and that's why we talk of *sound waves*."

"But why don't those waves hit one another and cause a fearful jumble?" Bill asked.

"The reason," Mr. Hinkley explained, "is that every sound has its own number of vibrations per second." By holding a hand up to his mouth and saying various words, Bill could feel this difference. Because the human voice acts this way, Alexander Graham Bell could invent the telephone.

SOUND MOVES LIKE A BOUNCING BALL

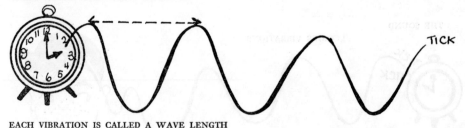

EACH VIBRATION IS CALLED A WAVE LENGTH

## Curious Alexander Bell

"Bell was a curious fellow," Mr. Hinkley said, "who threw cats out of windows to see why they always landed on four feet. He measured the light on fireflies. But his one great purpose in life was to teach deaf people how to speak. He didn't know much about electricity. Oh, he knew how an electromagnet made a doorbell ring. He knew that the telegraph worked on the same principle. The sending key was like the button on the doorbell. Pressed down, the key sent an electric current over a wire to a receiver where an electromagnet clicked a bar. The bar gave back a short dot or a long dash depending on how the sending key was pushed."

Bell thought that if he could make his deaf pupils see the vibration of human tones, he could teach them to speak by duplicating those vibrations. What he needed, Bell decided, was some kind of telegraph apparatus that could send a number of messages over a wire at one time. With the help of Thomas A. Watson, a young mechanic, Bell worked on the idea for almost four years.

Then one June day in 1874, Bell stood by the receiver trying to hear the signal Watson was sending from another room. The receiver gave a low twang. Bell rushed into the other room, shouting: "What did you do then?" All he had done, a surprised Watson responded, was to twang the points of a spring that had stuck together and closed the electric circuit. But Bell had heard that twang! With time and the right materials other tones—even human tones—could be sent over wires!

"Now," Mr. Hinkley said to Bill, "what happens when you speak into the mouthpiece of a telephone?"

"My voice gives off sound waves."

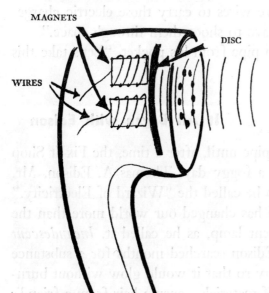

MAGNETS

WIRES

DISC

A TELEPHONE RECEIVER WORKS LIKE THIS: VIBRATING CURRENT, COMING THROUGH THE WIRES, HITS THE MAGNET, WHICH TOUCHES ANOTHER DISC AND MAKES IT VIBRATE TO MATCH THE SOUND WAVES THAT CAME INTO THE MOUTHPIECE.

THE DISC VIBRATES THE AIR AND YOU HEAR THESE VIBRATIONS.

"And suppose," Mr. Hinkley asked, "inside there is a thin disc, or *diaphragm*, that those sound waves hit?"

"Then," Bill answered, "the sound waves, hitting the disc, cause it to vibrate just as sound waves make a human ear vibrate."

Mr. Hinkley nodded. "Now beneath that disc are grains of carbon with an electric current passing through them. A loud sound wave presses the grains tight together. A lot of electricity passes through. But a soft sound moves the grains only slightly. A much smaller charge of electricity passes through."

Bill began to understand. "Loud sounds and soft sounds make the electric current vibrate as the voice does!"

"Good for you!" Mr. Hinkley cried. "And at the receiving end of the telephone this vibrating current hits a magnet which touches another disc. The magnet makes that disc vibrate by the amount of air it pushes against the disc. You hear those vibrations. In your ear they become the same sound waves that were spoken into the mouthpiece."

Bill could guess that a radio microphone acted like a telephone mouthpiece. "But you don't have wires to carry those electric charges in radio," he grumbled. "You have to shoot them through space."

Mr. Hinkley took a corncob pipe from his pocket. "Let's take this in easy stages," he said.

### It All Began with Edison

Mr. Hinkley puffed on the pipe until, after a time, the Fix-It Shop looked like a London street on a foggy day. Thomas A. Edison, Mr. Hinkley said finally, deserved to be called the "Wizard of Electricity." Of all Edison's inventions, none has changed our world more than the electric light—or the incandescent lamp, as he called it. *Incandescent* means *glowing with heat* and Edison searched months for a substance that he could heat with electricity so that it would glow without burning to ash. He tried thousands of materials—even a hair from a friend's red beard—before he hit upon carbon.

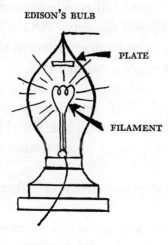

EDISON'S BULB

PLATE

FILAMENT

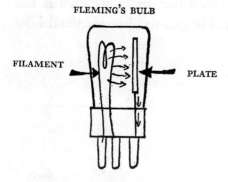

FLEMING'S BULB

FILAMENT

PLATE

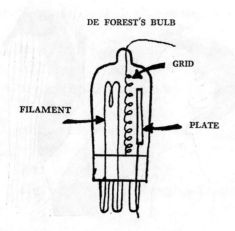

DE FOREST'S BULB

GRID

FILAMENT

PLATE

"Now," Mr. Hinkley said, "the carbon wire that glowed **for forty** hours in Edison's first successful incandescent lamp is called a filament. A little later, by inserting a metal plate inside his lamp, Edison produced a strange effect. When the current was turned on, the lamp glowed. Yet only when the plate carried a plus charge of electricity did the current move to any great extent."

"Then the filament was giving off a minus charge," Bill declared.

"And both the filament and the plate received that minus charge," Mr. Hinkley said. "When a current passes from plus to minus, it moves in two directions and we call it an *alternating current*. But an Englishman, Sir John A. Fleming, made a lamp, or vacuum tube, that allowed a current to pass only when the filament and plate both carried minus charges. When a current passes from minus to minus, it moves in one direction and is called a *direct current*, so what Fleming had discovered was the *rectifying* tube, so called because it changes *alternating* current into *direct* current."

Then an American, Lee De Forest, made a wonderful discovery. "You turn those slats on the Venetian blinds," Mr. Hinkley told Bill. Of course Bill could shut out or let in more sunlight, depending on how he turned the slats. "And what Lee De Forest did," Mr. Hinkley explained, "was to place between the filament and plate of the tube a small screen of wire, called a *grid*, that acted like those Venetian blinds."

Bill at first failed to see how the grid could control the number of minus charges passing between the filament and the plate. Mr. Hinkley chuckled. "Suppose that grid carried a plus charge; wouldn't those minus electrons move faster?" Bill nodded. "And if those electrons represented radio signals, wouldn't they grow stronger?" Again Bill nodded.

"The fancy way to say it is that those signals had been amplified," Mr. Hinkley said. And Mr. Hinkley added that he didn't care if Bill forgot about those tubes for a moment. He had fixed in his mind how they worked.

Mr. Hinkley held up the bowl of his corncob pipe. "Think of this as a microphone," he said. "Say something."

"My name is Bill," the boy replied.

"Good. The microphone changes the sound waves of your voice into electrical waves, just as a telephone mouthpiece does. To make sure those electrical waves do the job ahead of them, *amplifying tubes* make them stronger—sometimes as much as thirty trillion times stronger. If you are broadcasting 'My name is Bill' over a network that has stations in many cities, what happens now?"

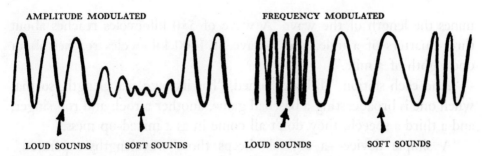

AMPLITUDE MODULATED       FREQUENCY MODULATED

LOUD SOUNDS    SOFT SOUNDS    LOUD SOUNDS    SOFT SOUNDS

Bill said he didn't know. Mr. Hinkley wasn't surprised, because many people didn't realize that these electrical waves were carried over telephone wires to the stations in various cities that would use them. Each station had to put those electrical waves into other waves that would shoot them through space, and that was why a *radio wave* was also called a *carrier wave*.

First, Mr. Hinkley said, Bill should understand how a radio wave acted, and the important thing was not to let strange words confuse him. "There are two kinds of radio waves, *AM* and *FM*. If loud sounds become big waves and little sounds become small waves, then you have AM broadcasting. The *A* stands for *Amplitude*, meaning that waves have been made stronger, and the *M* stands for *Modulating*, which means that the size of the wave has been fitted to the size of the electrical charge. In FM broadcasting, the *F* stands for *Frequency*, meaning that for loud sounds more waves are made and for low sounds fewer waves are made."

"So that *size* makes *AM* and *number* makes *FM*," Bill said.

Mr. Hinkley nodded. "AM or FM, a radio wave behaves the same. Most radio and television stations use AM waves, so those are what I'll explain first: A radio wave vibrates. It moves back and forth, making a *cycle*. And radio waves are measured by the number of cycles they make every second, which in AM broadcasting ranges from 550,000 to 1,600,000 cycles a second. For the sake of convenience we use the Greek word for one thousand, *kilo*, and reduce these big figures to *kilocycles* of from 550 to 1600—the figures you find on the dial of an AM radio set. The number of vibrations or cycles per second determines the length of the wave. A wave of 550 kilocycles reaches about three-quarters of a mile, and a wave of 1600 kilocycles reaches about one-eighth of a mile."

"And each station," Bill exclaimed, "has its own wavelength, so that when one is broadcasting a baseball game, another a rock and roll singer, and a third a speech, they don't all come in as a mixed-up mess."

"A simple device—a crystal—keeps those wavelengths separated," Mr. Hinkley said. "The thickness of the crystal determines the number of cycles in each radio wave. So one station uses a crystal that gives it a wavelength of 550 and another a crystal that gives a wavelength of 660 or 770 or 1320 on up to 1600."

"How is FM broadcasting different?" Bill asked.

"FM waves operate in such rapid cycles—usually between 54,000,-000 and 216,000,000 cycles every second—that we use the Greek word *mega*, meaning *million*, for them, and speak of them as *mega-cycles* rather than kilocycles. Stations that broadcast FM waves each have their own *frequency*, rather than wavelength, so it is possible for a station to do AM and FM broadcasting at the same time. The advantage of FM broadcasting is that you get less interference from static and more faithful reproduction of sound, so that it is especially good for broadcasting music."

### Sending a Radio Wave

Bill recalled a day driving in the country with his parents when he had seen a radio transmitting station. He knew now why the broadcasting studio could be miles away from its radio-transmitting station, since telephone wires carried to the transmitter the electrical charges produced in the microphone. But what then?

Mr. Hinkley asked if Bill remembered the tower at that station. "Two wires," he said, "run up that tower and are connected to a generator that produces alternating current. One wire carries a plus charge and the other a minus charge, and the air between them is called an *electrostatic field.* All this means is that if the generator producing the current dies down to zero, the electrostatic field loses its force and the electricity in the air rushes back toward the wires. But now the generator plays a trick. It starts again, and the wire that was plus it makes minus and the wire that was minus it makes plus. So the electrical charge which a fraction of a wink before was a minus charge pulled toward a plus wire is now a minus charge being pushed away by a minus wire. Off it pops into space—a radio wave! The generator repeats this trick many times every second."

"But how," Bill asked, "do those waves know where to go?"

Whence could they go, Mr. Hinkley wanted to know, except along the ground or into the sky? "When they are *ground waves,* hitting buildings or mountains or other obstacles, they do what might be expected—they grow weaker the farther they travel. So, for best results, a radio wave is bounced off the sky."

"'Bounced off the sky,'" Bill repeated. "What do you think is up there—a wall?"

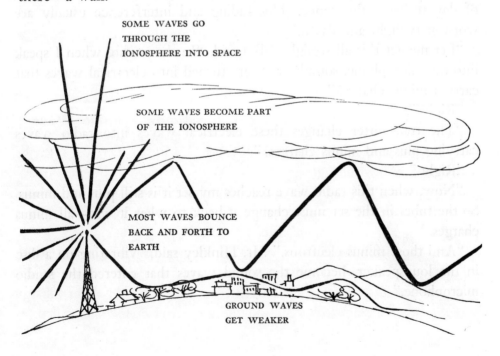

SOME WAVES GO
THROUGH THE
IONOSPHERE INTO SPACE

SOME WAVES BECOME PART
OF THE IONOSPHERE

MOST WAVES BOUNCE
BACK AND FORTH TO
EARTH

GROUND WAVES
GET WEAKER

## Mr. Hinkley's Wall in the Sky

"Of course there is a wall up there," Mr. Hinkley retorted. "It is the upper layer of the air called the *ionosphere.*

"In fact," Mr. Hinkley added, "it's a movable wall of air. You can never be certain how far from the earth you'll find the ionosphere, for rays from the sun tend to push it down. During the day the ionosphere may be fifty miles from the earth and, at night, without the sun's rays, the ionosphere may be two hundred miles away.

"Now," Mr. Hinkley continued, "when a radio wave strikes the ionosphere three things happen. Some of the wave goes through into outer space. Some of the wave becomes part of the ionosphere. But most of the wave bounces back to earth."

"Sometimes when I'm listening to a radio program it seems to fade away," Bill said. "Why is that?"

"With the ionosphere moving up and down," Mr. Hinkley replied, "*sky waves* fade or pick up interference from ground waves. The time of day makes a difference. This fading and interference usually are worst at twilight and dawn."

"Let me get this all straight," Bill said. "In the studio, when I speak into the microphone, sound waves are turned into electrical waves that carry a minus charge?"

"Right."

"The transmitter changes these electrical waves into radio waves carrying plus and minus charges?"

"Right."

"Now, when this radio wave reaches my set it is still plus and minus. So the tubes in the set must change it back to what it was—all minus charges."

"And those minus electrons," Mr. Hinkley said, "vibrating on a disc in the loudspeaker, become the sound waves that entered the studio microphone."

"Well, I'll be darned!" Bill grinned. After a moment, he asked: "Are the pictures I see on that television screen sent the same way?"

"As far as the carrier waves that bring the pictures to the television set are concerned, yes."

"Even moving pictures?" Bill insisted.

"Who says a picture can move?" Mr. Hinkley demanded.

"I do," Bill said. "I've seen 'em move!"

## A Horse Takes Its Own Picture

Mr. Hinkley chuckled and sorted through the tools on his workbench until he found a flashlight. He switched on the light and held it before Bill's eyes. After a time he switched it off, asking: "Do you see the light?"

"Sure."

"But it isn't there."

"Then why do I still see it?"

The answer, Mr. Hinkley explained, was what scientists called *persistence of vision*. The eyes retain an image of an object for a short period after it disappears. He asked Bill to remember that fact while he told him a story about a horse.

"Many years ago in California," Mr. Hinkley continued, "a group of gentlemen had a heated argument over whether a horse, when running, ever lifts all four feet off the ground at one time. Some swore it did and others were stubbornly sure it didn't. Finally, one of the men went to a photographer—an Englishman named Eadweard Muybridge—to settle the dispute for them. Muybridge placed twenty-four cameras in a row, and from the lens shutter of each, stretched a thread across the track. When the horse ran, he would break the threads and take his own picture."

"Well," Bill blurted, "did the horse ever take all four feet off the ground at once?"

THE HORSE BROKE THE THREADS AND TOOK HIS OWN PICTURE

"Yes, it did," Mr. Hinkley admitted. "Newspapers everywhere gave attention to what Muybridge had discovered. He became a sensation. But what nobody knew then was that if Muybridge's twenty-four pictures could have been taken in one second, and then shown to you in one second, you would have seen that horse *running*."

"But in *each* of those pictures," Bill said, "that horse wasn't moving!"

"Yet your *persistence of vision* would have made you see a running horse." Mr. Hinkley laughed. "When you go to the movies, or see a movie on television, the screen is actually dark twenty-four times every second—you pay to see nothing at all then—except that your eyes still see the last picture and then the next picture without noticing the dark screen."

"So motion pictures are all kind of a hocus-pocus!" Bill exclaimed.

"Really a trick of the eyes," Mr. Hinkley agreed.

### How Television Works

Once you understood the principles behind radio, Mr. Hinkley said, television didn't have to be any mystery. You had two new problems to solve:

First, you had to take the light and dark parts of a picture and change them into electrical charges.

Second, in order to give motion you had to send a number of pictures every second, and in most television systems that number varied from twenty-four to thirty pictures every second.

"The wonder of the whole process," Mr. Hinkley said, "is the television camera. Its lens draws in, or focuses, the light rays received from an object. Inside the camera is an electron tube called an *orthicon*. When the light rays pass through the lens into the orthicon, they fall on a sensitive screen which is coated with a material that can change light into electricity. There are thousands of these tiny squares of light-sensitive material. Now what has to happen, if television is to work, when light falls on one of these squares?"

"It has to give off a minus charge of electricity," Bill stated.

"That's right—and the more light that falls on any area of the mosaic, the more minus electrons must be given off." It also stood to reason, Mr. Hinkley added, that there had to be some place for those electrons to go, and so behind the mosaic was a plate called the *target* to which those minus charges were sent.

"At the other end of the orthicon," Mr. Hinkley continued, "is an *electron gun*, and its job is to shoot off a steady stream of electrons so that they form a regular pattern on the target. Here, let me draw you a picture of the whole orthicon." And Mr. Hinkley's picture looked like this:

THE CAMERA TUBE IS AN ORTHICON

1. LIGHT FALLS ON
   A SENSITIVE SCREEN

2. WHICH RELEASES ELECTRONS TO THE
   TARGET

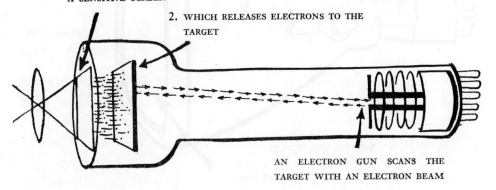

AN ELECTRON GUN SCANS THE
TARGET WITH AN ELECTRON BEAM

"That electron gun," Mr. Hinkley said, "is between two sets of coils, each worked by magnetism at tremendous speed. One set moves a beam of electrons up and down and the other set moves a beam of electrons from side to side. One line of the picture at a time is swept by a beam, and whenever it touches the sensitive element giving off electrons it sends back electrons to the target. In ordinary television a picture will have 525 lines, and the beam covers or *scans* as many as thirty such pictures every second!"

"You can't call an orthicon a lazy fellow," Bill remarked.

Mr. Hinkley agreed. "Nor could you call the radio wave that carries these electrical charges lazy. It does two jobs at once. It takes the electrical impulses given by the light (called *video* after the Latin for *I see*) and combines them with the electrical impulses given by the sound (called *audio* after the Latin for *I hear*).

"You know," Mr. Hinkley said, "in order to give you thirty pictures a second, your home receiving set can get as many as 4,000,000 electrical impulses in that second. Each comes to you as a light dot or a dark dot. But all you see is a complete picture."

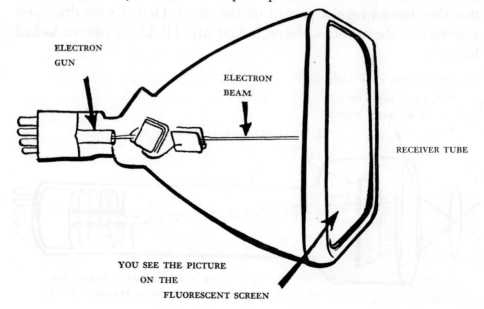

ELECTRON
GUN

ELECTRON
BEAM

RECEIVER TUBE

YOU SEE THE PICTURE
ON THE
FLUORESCENT SCREEN

## Unscrambling 4,000,000 Dots

Bill poked his nose into the back of the television set Mr. Hinkley was repairing. "Just think," he said, "of all those tubes unscrambling as many as 4,000,000 dots every second!"

"Chiefly," Mr. Hinkley told him, "the job is done by an electronic tube called the *cathode-ray* tube or the *receiver* tube. There is also an electron gun in that tube. Exactly as the electron gun does in the orthicon of the television camera, the electron gun in the receiver tube of your television set shoots a constant stream of electrons over the surface of the picture tube. This time the electrons hit a fluorescent screen with a sensitive material that gives off greater or lesser amounts of light. The beam of the electron gun in the receiver tube must be perfectly timed with the beam in the orthicon to keep the picture from going out of focus."

"That makes the picture then?" Bill asked. "I mean, the beam from the electron gun lighting up a series of brighter or darker spots on a fluorescent screen?"

Mr. Hinkley nodded.

"And that can happen 4,000,000 times a second?"

"It can."

"And I suppose that each television station has its own wavelength?"

"Its own *frequency*," Mr. Hinkley corrected. "Television stations use FM waves."

"Then," Bill said, "you can have several television channels operating at once as long as each keeps within its own megacycles?"

"That's the idea."

"But how long does it take," Bill asked, "from the time a program is broadcast until I see and hear it?"

"Well," Mr. Hinkley replied, "suppose you were at a concert, sitting in the last row of a big theater, and I was at home listening to the same concert on television or radio. I would hear the concert before you did."

"Go on!" Bill guessed that he knew when Mr. Hinkley was pulling his leg.

"But I would," Mr. Hinkley insisted. "Sound travels at the rate of 1,120 feet every second. But a radio wave travels at the speed of light, which is 186,000 miles a second—or better than seven times around the world!"

## An Owl with a Tummyache

Bill shook his head, thinking it was no wonder that light—or anything traveling that fast—played tricks with your eyes, and that pictures that weren't moving seemed to be moving. "Mr. Hinkley," Bill declared, "we live in a wonderful world!"

"We do indeed," the man agreed.

"I'll tell you one thing," Bill said. "I just hope you get our television set repaired so that we can use it tonight."

"All I've got to do is stop talking to you to make it," Mr. Hinkley reminded his caller.

"Well, I can get out, so don't blame me if you don't," Bill said with a chuckle.

For a moment, peering over the rim of his glasses, the owner of the Fix-It Shop looked like an owl with a tummyache. Then tiny, crinkling lines formed at the corners of Mr. Hinkley's mouth and in another moment he broke into a grin.

## 3. HEAT: Man's Warm-hearted Friend

"GOLLY, it's hot!" Bill complained when he came out of school.

Over his shoulder a pleasant voice said: "The sun's surely boiling down today."

Bill turned. He liked Miss Pringle. Oh, she was a teacher who made him work—there was no silly cutting-up in Miss Pringle's classes—but she was even-tempered, fair, a good sport. Bill said, "I'll walk to the railroad station with you." Then, squinting up at the sun again, he grumbled: "You wouldn't think a little blob like that could give off so much heat."

Miss Pringle laughed. "That 'little blob,'" she said, "is a million times larger than the earth. It's a good thing, too, that the sun's 93,-000,000 miles away, for its temperature is about 12,000 degrees Fahrenheit."

"When you reckon that water

boils at 212 degrees Fahrenheit," Bill said, "it's no wonder she's a scorcher."

"But think of what a wonderful friend heat is to us," Miss Pringle exclaimed. "It keeps us warm in winter, cooks our food, makes plants grow, lights our homes, drives our automobiles, trains, and airplanes."

Bill nodded. "I guess it would be a funny world without that furnace up there in the sky."

"Indeed it would," Miss Pringle agreed. "Without the sun the earth would become a dead planet like the moon."

Miss Pringle reacted the way she always did. Just as a person could be a natural baseball player, Miss Pringle was a natural teacher. Let her see that a pupil was interested in a subject, and off she raced—like a good outfielder at the crack of a bat.

### What Heat Is

Everything around Bill, Miss Pringle said, was composed of particles called *molecules*. These particles, or molecules, constantly moved about, and it was this motion that gave us *kinetic energy* or heat.

"What's that again?" demanded a puzzled Bill. "I mean, this 'kinetic energy' stuff."

Miss Pringle smiled. "Walking along the street with me," she explained, "you use kinetic energy. *Kinetic* is a word the Greeks gave us. It means *to move*. And that's what heat is—a form of movement. The more motion molecules make, the more heat they give. Now if the temperature of the water were the same in a pond and a lake, which would give off more heat?"

"The lake," Bill said. "It's bigger."

"You're right! There are more molecules in the lake, more movement, and therefore more heat. Any form of energy that is electrical, chemical, or mechanical can be turned into heat," Bill's teacher said.

"Even ice?"

"Of course! Rub two ice cubes together and see if the heat doesn't make them melt. Producing heat this way—by *friction*—is one of man's oldest discoveries. The Indians, I'm sure you know, rubbed sticks together to make a fire."

At that moment an automobile drove by, its brake bands smoking. "There's another example of heat produced by friction," Miss Pringle said with a laugh.

"How else do we get heat?" Bill asked.

"Well," Miss Pringle told him, "first *from the sun*—the heat that makes plants grow. And *from the interior of earth*—the lava in a volcano proves that. And *from electricity*"—as Bill knew from touching light bulbs that had been burning for some time. "And *from gases*—which, when compressed, give off heat.

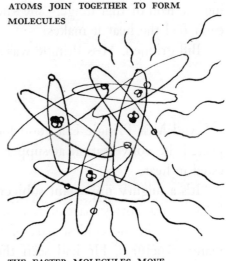

ATOMS JOIN TOGETHER TO FORM MOLECULES

THE FASTER MOLECULES MOVE, THE MORE HEAT THEY MAKE

"The wonderful thing about energy," Bill's teacher went on, "is that you can change it into something else but you can never destroy it. But when you do change energy from one form to another, then you get heat."

"You burn wood and get ashes," Bill said, trying to understand.

"What actually happens," Miss Pringle explained, "is that the oxygen in the air joins with the fuel and forms a new material called carbon dioxide. When water freezes, becoming ice, it gives off heat. And when water boils it changes into steam."

"So that changing a thing into something else is the trick that causes heat?" Bill suggested.

"That's the trick," Miss Pringle agreed, "but the way the change is made is also important." They had reached the railroad station, and Miss Pringle pointed to the rusty hinge on the door. "Oxygen is changing the iron of that hinge," she said, "but changing it so slowly that we can't feel the heat it makes."

Bill grinned. Miss Pringle was a good talker.

## How Heat Works for Us

"And Miss Pringle is a good looker, too," Father said when Bill repeated the conversation at supper. Father was glad that Bill was interested in heat.

"It's a mighty important subject," Father said. "If you measured our house in the hottest part of summer, you would find that the house was taller than in the coldest part of winter." Bill knew that heat expands many structures. He had seen the iron bolts in bridges that made it possible for them to grow longer in hot weather.

"All gases, and almost all solids and liquids, expand when heated," Father said.

"The way the mercury in our thermometer expands when the heat from the inside of the mouth strikes it," Mother added. "We can measure temperature by it because mercury expands so evenly."

"That's a good point," Father said. "Heat works in different ways. When air is heated, it grows lighter and rises so that in winter a room is warmer at the ceiling than on the floor. Copper expands more than iron at the same temperature. Alcohol boils at a lower temperature than water and water boils at a lower temperature than the mercury in a thermometer."

"Can we use this knowledge?" Bill asked.

Father nodded. "Take crude oil," he said. "Crude oil is actually a mixture of gasoline, kerosene, and heavy oils. With heat, each can be separated from the others."

"You mean, because each boils at a different temperature?"

"Exactly," Father answered. "If you want to remove the kerosene from the crude oil, you heat it to a temperature that makes the kerosene rise in a vapor (as boiling water, changing into steam, rises in a vapor).

Then the vapor made by the boiling kerosene is passed through cold pipes—called *condensers*—that turn the vapor back into kerosene. At other temperatures the gasoline and heavy oils can be removed in the same way."

"It's like a magic show!" Bill exclaimed.

## Or a Three-ring Circus

"In using heat," Father said, "man is really the master over a three-ring circus." What Father meant was that there are three ways in which heat can be made to travel. No matter how heat moves, man can put it to work.

IN CONDUCTION, THE HEAT PASSES FROM MOLECULE TO MOLECULE OF A SOLID. YOU HEAT A PAN BY CONDUCTION

A STOVE (OR RADIATOR) HEATS THE AIR AROUND IT BY CONVECTION

THE HOT AIR RISES AND THE COLD AIR PUSHES IN UNDERNEATH

"When you hold an iron over a flame," Father said, "the flame passes the heat from molecule to molecule. Thus, if the iron is held in the flame long enough, the molecules will pass the heat from

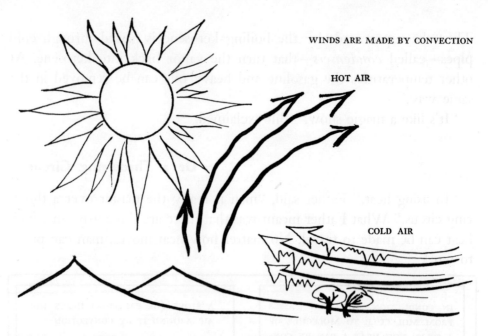

WINDS ARE MADE BY CONVECTION

HOT AIR

COLD AIR

end to end. When heat travels in this way, the process is known as *conduction*.

"When you heat a stove," Father continued, "another process is involved. The stove makes the air around it warmer, and since warm air is always lighter than cold air, the cold air pushes the warm air away from the stove. But now this cold air grows warmer and lighter and is in turn shoved aside by another wave of cold air."

"So that a regular current of hot and cold air is flowing through the room!" Bill exclaimed.

"Good boy!" Father said approvingly. "When heat travels by being moved from one place to another in this manner, the process is called *convection*."

Mother declared that she could give an example of convection on a larger scale. "After all, the sun does not heat all parts of the earth equally, so the cold air and warm air, pushing each other, form the winds."

Father nodded and asked Bill, "What makes an object cold?"

"I guess it's not being warm," Bill said, feeling that was a silly answer.

But it wasn't. The absence of heat is all that makes things cold. And since heat will always move toward a cold object, if you want to keep a place warm you have to use something to keep heat from moving away.

"We use *insulators* to do that," Father said. "When we built our house, we put a material called rock wool between the outer and inner walls because rock wool is an insulator. It cuts down the movement of air, or blocks it like a tackle or guard stops a ball-carrier in a football game. So in winter this insulation helps to keep the hot air in, and in summer it helps to keep the hot air out."

Bill grinned. "It's still like a football game, only the teams have changed goals!" But Father had said heat traveled in three ways and had described only two—conduction and convection. "What's the third way that heat travels?" Bill asked.

"By *radiation*," Father answered. He told Bill to think once more of the sun shining down on the earth. "What if clouds get in the way? Now the heat waves are cut off. The clouds can absorb them, but the clouds also can bounce the heat waves in many directions. So the heat travels on—and *has* to travel on, since we know that heat always travels toward cold until both areas reach the same temperature."

Bill asked: "Can you stop heat from traveling by radiation?"

"In two ways," Father said. "You can absorb the heat as the clouds sometimes do. Or you can reflect heat waves, which is the job done by the shining surface inside a thermos bottle."

Bill looked around the room.

HEAT TRAVELS BY RADIATION

There was the lighted bulb in the floor lamp, and inside that bulb heat traveled the length of the filament by conduction. It had been a warm day, and yet the house was cool—thanks to the insulation in the walls that blocked the heat outside from traveling by convection into the room where they were having supper. And of course he had left his lunch box with its thermos bottle on a chair instead of putting it away, but now he knew why his soup had been hot at noon.

A three-ring circus, sure enough, going on right under his nose. "Live and learn," he said cheerfully.

### Early Steam Engines

When Bill reached school next morning, he found that Miss Pringle had arrived earlier than usual. She had been busy, too, for the blackboard was covered with drawings. Miss Pringle explained to the class how, on the way to the railroad station the day before, she and Bill had talked about the sun as the warm-hearted servant of man. She had thought about the subject all last evening. Most of all, she had thought of how man had learned to use heat to lessen his burdens.

"What happens when we boil water?" Miss Pringle asked.

Blue-eyed Kathie Wilson answered: "We get steam."

"But suppose we trap the steam in a boiler," Miss Pringle continued. "When it is cooled, it condenses, or takes less space. The empty place that now exists in the boiler we call a vacuum.

"In 1601," the teacher said, "an Italian named Giovanni Battista della Porta thought, 'You can't have a vacuum like that. Nature won't let you. When the steam cools and forms a vacuum, other water can be sucked up into that empty space!' So Della Porta hit upon the idea for the first primitive steam engine—really a pump—though he never actually built one. For the next century, many persons, using Della Porta's idea, invented various kinds of crude steam engines that would drain the water out of deep mines. The most successful of these inventors was an English blacksmith, Thomas Newcomen."

Miss Pringle turned to her first drawing. "As you can see," she said, "Newcomen built a fire under a boiler. Above the boiler he placed this rod—or piston—which was attached to this pump-handle. Now notice this tube which enters the boiler directly beneath the piston. Through this tube Newcomen could send a fine stream of cold water into the boiler. The cold water cooled the steam and formed a vacuum. Now what would the weight of the air in the piston-chamber do?"

"Make the piston move down?" Bill volunteered.

"By forcing it down?" Miss Pringle insisted.

"Yes," Bill answered. "It would be forced down. And since the pump-handle is attached to it, the handle would move up."

"But now your water is cool," Miss Pringle continued. "How can you make your engine pump more water?"

A dozen hands were raised and the teacher called on red-headed Tom Blake. "You'd have to heat the water so that you'd have more steam to cool," Tom said.

"But wouldn't that use up a lot of steam and fuel?"

"It sure would," Tom declared.

### Enter James Watt

Newcomen's engine had been in use for about sixty years, when a maker of mathematical instruments for the University of Glasgow wondered about this waste of fuel. With true Scottish common sense, James Watt liked to get a penny's worth for a penny spent. The trouble with Newcomen's contraption, Watt reasoned, was that the cylinder containing the water and the piston chamber were both cooled. Why couldn't they be divided, so that the cylinder always remained hot while the piston-chamber was cooled? The answer was a saving of three-quarters of the fuel cost in operating the engine! Time also was saved. And the quicker the water could be pumped out of a mine, the more money the miners and mine owners could make.

"Since the pressure of the air, or atmosphere, actually forced down the piston," Miss Pringle said, "for a long time people called Watt's contraption an *atmospheric engine*. The first Watt engine was used to

*Watt's first Engine*

pump out a tin mine. Watching it thump away, people began to wonder what else you could do with an engine like that. Old Newcomen's engine had worked too slowly to seem much good for anything except pumping, but Watt's engine had a lot of life to it. Suppose you could put that to-and-fro movement of the piston to other uses. For example, could a crank be attached to that piston so a wheel would turn?"

"Sure it could . . . sure it could!" shouted a dozen voices, with Bill's voice as loud as any.

Miss Pringle quieted the class, but she smiled, too. Did they truly realize what that idea had meant? Before the main source of power for turning a wheel had been the wind or water, and of course for mills or factories water had been the only reliable source of power. So mills and factories had appeared in only those areas where there were rivers and falls. Only a few products could be manufactured, and a few people hold jobs, and less money was available to buy what the farmer raised or the craftsman made with his own hands.

"But now," Miss Pringle said, "Watt's engine meant that you could build factories anywhere. You no longer needed a river for a mill that could weave cotton or woolen cloth. And the more steam engines you built, the more coal you needed to heat them, so the miners prospered also. And if you could turn a wheel in a factory—"

Miss Pringle paused. Bill could feel his excitement growing. Whenever Miss Pringle taught a lesson like this, she always ended by playing "You Name It!" Everyone in the class would be given a chance to cry out the name of one invention that had resulted because a steam engine could be made to turn a wheel.

Kathie Wilson started: "You could drive a carriage and get rid of horses."

"You could build railroads," Tom Blake added.

"And turn the paddlewheel on a boat," Bill said when his turn came.

Tom Blake waved his hand as though he had springs in his arm. "Miss Pringle," he called, "I want to know about the engine that drives our car."

## The Gasoline Engine

The teacher laughed. The class, she declared, was pulling her leg, for they knew perfectly well that she had intended giving them a spelling test this morning. "A small steam engine," she said, "cannot do the work of a big steam engine. Yet a small gasoline engine is often as good at producing power as a large one. As early as 1820 an Englishman named Cecil built a gasoline engine, but not until the present century did the gasoline engine catch on in America.

"A gasoline engine," Miss Pringle said, "is called an *internal-combustion engine*, which means only that it is powered by the explosion of gasoline vapor. How many of you know where the carburetor is in your family's automobile?"

Bill's hand was one of the six raised.

"And the spark plugs?"

Four more hands shot up.

Miss Pringle smiled.

"In the carburetor," she explained, "a vacuum draws in air, and that air in turn forms a vacuum around the opening to the gasoline tank. So what has to happen?"

"You can't have a vacuum," Bill said. "Gasoline has to be sucked up into the carburetor."

"Where it mixes with the air and forms a mist," Miss Pringle went on. "Valves permit the gasoline and air to pass into a cylinder where a piston is located. And in that cylinder are two points, one plus and one minus, so that electricity can be passed between them."

Miss Pringle said they had to think for a moment of their car battery, where the electric current was made. This current was carried to the spark plug that shot it between the + and — points in the cylinder with the piston, thus exploding the vapory mixture of gasoline and air. Down drops the piston, which turns a crankshaft, which in turn spins a long metal rod, which turns the axle to which the wheels are connected.

A GASOLINE ENGINE LOOKS LIKE THIS

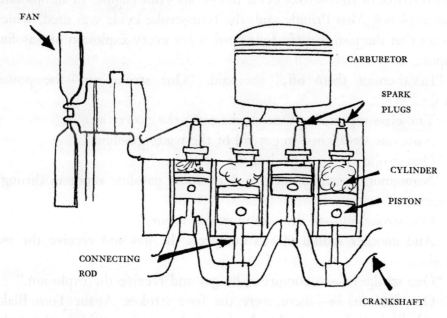

FAN

CARBURETOR

SPARK
PLUGS

CYLINDER

PISTON

CONNECTING
ROD

CRANKSHAFT

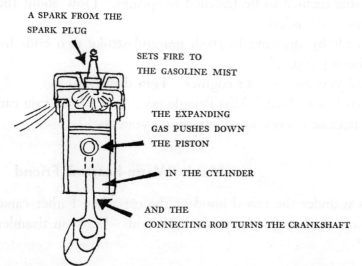

A SPARK FROM THE
SPARK PLUG

SETS FIRE TO
THE GASOLINE MIST

THE EXPANDING
GAS PUSHES DOWN
THE PISTON

IN THE CYLINDER

AND THE
CONNECTING ROD TURNS THE CRANKSHAFT

It all sounded easy when you said it quickly, Miss Pringle admitted. But a great deal of careful planning and craftsmanship had to go into building a gasoline engine. First, you had to decide whether you wanted a two-stroke or four-stroke cycle to operate your engine. In automobiles and airplanes, Miss Pringle said, the four-stroke cycle was used, which meant that the piston made four strokes for every explosion of gasoline vapor.

"Let's count them off," she said. "One stroke out—the power stroke."

The class repeated: "One stroke out—the power stroke."

"Now one stroke in—to get rid of the waste gasoline."

"One stroke in—to get rid of the waste gas."

"Now another stroke out—to draw more gasoline vapor in through a vacuum."

"One stroke out—to draw in more gas vapor."

"And another stroke in—to compress the gas and receive the explosion."

"One stroke in—to compress the gas and receive the explosion."

Out, in, out, in—there were the four strokes. Again Tom Blake waved the arm that seemed to be fastened to springs. "How about the two-stroke engine?" he asked.

"Stroke one ends by drawing in fresh gas and stroke two ends by getting rid of the waste gas."

"Where would you use such an engine?" Tom demanded.

"On an outboard motorboat," Miss Pringle said, "and I hope you can spell motorboat because it's one of the words on your test!"

### Man's Warm-hearted Friend

Bill's head was under the raised hood of the car when Father came home that evening. Rather grumpily, the man said: "What in thunder are you doing?"

"Looking."

"For your baseball bat? That's in the attic."

Bill grinned. He wanted to find out if Miss Pringle was right— about the carburetor and spark plugs and that stuff.

"Raising kids!" Father complained with a sigh. "It's a wonder they ever grow up with noses, considering where they insist on sticking them!"

But Father was pleased with Bill's interest. The more cylinders the engine had, he explained, the more power it had. "Of course they are timed," Father said, "so that one of them explodes while the others are filling up with gasoline. In a four-cylinder engine, one piston is making the power stroke at every moment in the four-stroke cycle."

Bill shook his head, filled with wonder. Millions of years ago, man had known that the sun was his friend, and some people, believing the sun was a god, had become sun-worshipers. But in time man had learned to make his own heat through friction, and then he had learned how heat traveled and had put that knowledge to work. Della Porta's idea for a pump had been improved by old Thomas Newcomen, and then James Watt had been shocked by the waste of so much steam and fuel and had divided the chambers of his engine, and then Watt's piston had been attached to a crank so that it could turn a wheel, and here was an automobile as one result of that chain of events! You turned an idea loose in the world and where it was going to end nobody knew! Science in a way was a big, continuous game of men saying, "Work this gadget a little differently, and see what happens!"

There wasn't anything on television that the family wanted to see, so after supper Bill suggested they play "Let's Name It!" for all the ways in which heat was used as man's warm-hearted servant.

Mother named things that she knew about: heating homes, in baking and cooking, for lights, and even for the treatment of diseases with sunlamps and X-ray machines.

And Father named the things that would occur to a businessman: in smelting ores, refining oils, and driving trucks and tractors.

And Bill cried, "And growing plants— Which reminds me! I want to visit Uncle John on his farm this summer."

"So that you can drive his tractor," guessed Father, who was nobody's fool.

## 4. FOOD : The World's Harvests on Our Tables

UNCLE John was as good a farmer as Miss Pringle was a teacher.

"There's nothing better a man can be," he told Bill proudly. "Until you had farmers, people wandered around the world searching for food like a pack of animals."

But that was long ago, Bill insisted, and Uncle John answered: "Yes, thousands and thousands of years ago when there weren't as many people in the world as you find today in one big city."

PICTURES LEFT BY PRIMITIVE MAN ON THE WALLS OF CAVES

"Before there were farmers," said Uncle John, "everybody lived a hard existence. The men hunted and fished. The women dug for roots or searched the forests for berries and herbs. A great many people died from starvation. The pictures left by primitive man on the walls of his cave show how he trapped and killed wild animals. No event was more important in his life—in fact, the struggle to find enough food the year round *was* his life.

"Think of how different our world is!" Uncle John exclaimed. "When we have supper, we won't eat only the vegetables and meat we raise ourselves. We may drink tea from India, or China, or coffee from Brazil. Our food will be seasoned with spices from the East Indies. The flour in the cake may come from Kansas and the oranges in the filling from California or Florida." Uncle John laughed. "You know what I told the grocer in the village? 'Folks can talk about that United Nations building in New York,' I said, 'but your store was a United Nations building before that one was thought of!'"

## How It All Started

Sitting on the front porch and smelling supper cooking in the kitchen, Bill felt the tug of his growing appetite. "People take food for granted," he said to Uncle John. "They don't know what real hunger is."

"That's not true," Unce John commented. "In some parts of Australia you can find natives who hunt and grub for roots and berries just like those poor devils in the old Stone Age. And in lots of areas in the world, there are people going hungry because they don't know farming as a science."

Bill frowned. "How did we first learn to be farmers?"

"Mostly by accident," Uncle John said. "In ancient times, when a good crop of grass was found, the women scattered seeds on the ground as an offering to the gods. When they came back the following year, they found more grass growing, and so in time they learned that by sowing seeds they could grow crops."

At that moment the story of man changed. To be a farmer, man had to care for his crops. He stopped being a wanderer. He built shelters, then villages, and where food became plentiful large communities developed.

"That happened in Egypt about six thousand years ago," Uncle John said. "Not only did the flood waters of the Nile River deposit rich soil

TO BE A FARMER, MAN HAD TO CARE FOR HIS CROPS

to grow plants, but the warm climate made it possible to harvest three crops every year. Those Egyptians raised many things we eat today—wheat, barley, beans, peas, radishes, lettuce, cabbage, cucumbers."

But Bill didn't think that was so strange. "I guess people always have eaten about the same things."

"Well, guess again!" Uncle John told him. "That wasn't true even in those days. While the Egyptians ate all those vegetables, John the Baptist had to survive in the desert on locusts and wild honey. And when Esau sold his birthright to Jacob for a mess of pottage, all he was getting was a thick soup made out of beans or lentils.

"In our own country," Uncle John continued, "we eat many things today that our forefathers never tasted." Grapefruit, avocados, loganberries, bananas, kumquats, mangos—these were some of the fruits Uncle John mentioned. And among the vegetables he included artichokes, soybeans, Chinese cabbage, broccoli, and Swiss chard.

## The Mystery of the Deserted Cities

"Every kind of food," Bill said, "could tell a story if it could talk."

"That is a fact," Uncle John admitted. He remembered, once when he attended a banquet, thinking that he could write a good history book around that meal. First they had served oysters, which the Romans had brought back from their invasion of the British Isles in the time of Caesar. And the cherries and peaches in the fruit salad made Uncle John recall that it had been the scarcity of food that had led the Greeks and Romans to wander all over the world. So they had found cherries in Persia and peaches in the Orient, cattle in France and grain in Egypt. And the spices in the main course at the banquet reminded Uncle John that when Columbus stumbled upon America he was seeking a short route to India because he wanted spices highly valued in preserving meat.

"Everybody likes to eat," Bill said with a laugh.

"Everybody *has* to," Uncle John retorted, and that started him on another story about the mystery of the deserted cities among the ancient Mayans. In the jungles of Central America explorers discovered whole cities that apparently had been abandoned for some strange reason. All the buildings looked as if they were in good shape, and yet one day the people had seemed to decide that they would quit the place. Some miles away they had built another city, lived there for a number of years, and then one day off they moved again. "Do you know why?" Uncle John asked.

Bill shook his head.

"Even though the Mayans knew how to raise corn and other vegetables, they did not know how to keep the soil from wearing out. When the land no longer gave the food they needed, they moved away, built a new city, and started over!"

"That was a hard way to run a country," Bill commented.

Next morning, tramping over the fields of the farm, Uncle John told Bill that a good farmer treats his plants almost as though they were his own children. In giving his plants every opportunity to grow, the farmer is like a faithful guardian. In protecting them from diseases, he

THE MAYANS DESERTED THEIR CITIES WHEN THE LAND WORE OUT

is like a wise doctor. And in safeguarding them from harmful insects, parasites, and other enemies, he is like a watchful policeman.

"You make it sound like a big job," Bill complained.

"It *is* a big job," Uncle John insisted. "A man needs a sound training to be a farmer these days. He has to know a lot—and, young fella, there's no better place to begin than by knowing how a plant grows."

## How a Plant Grows

Uncle John had Bill pull up a rye plant and examine its root hairs. Of course part of the root hairs remained in the soil, and that was the point Uncle John wanted to stress. "If you could measure the root hairs on a single rye plant, how far do you think they'd reach?"

Bill guessed: "Two or three feet."

"No," Uncle John said. "No matter how astonishing it seems, the total length of the root hairs of one rye plant can exceed five thousand miles! When you pull up a beet, what you hold in your hand is only part of a root system that could reach into the ground for ten feet. A cabbage plant can spread its roots over two hundred cubic feet."

Bill whistled. "There's a reason that happens!"

Uncle John nodded. "Roots absorb water for the plant, store food for it, and hold up the plant, among other functions. Every phase of a plant's growth is a wonderful discovery. Take the leaves, stem, and flowers, where you see the green parts of a plant," Uncle John said. "These parts contain *chlorophyll*, which means *light green leaf*. When the temperature is right, the sun falling on the leaf starts a chemical action by which

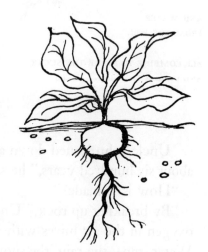

THE ROOTS SOAK UP WATER FOR THE PLANT, HOLD IT IN PLACE, AND STORE FOOD

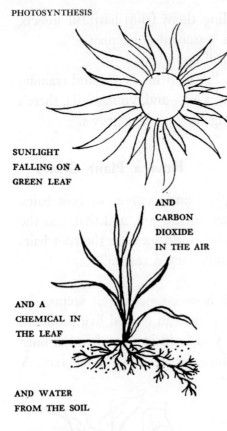

PHOTOSYNTHESIS

SUNLIGHT
FALLING ON A
GREEN LEAF

AND
CARBON
DIOXIDE
IN THE AIR

AND A
CHEMICAL IN
THE LEAF

AND WATER
FROM THE SOIL

ALL COMBINE TO MAKE THE SUGAR
AND STARCH THE PLANT NEEDS

water and carbon dioxide combine to manufacture the starches and sugars the plant needs."

"If the roots suck up water from the ground," Bill asked, "where does the carbon dioxide come from?"

"The air mostly," Uncle John replied. "We breathe out carbon dioxide. All animals do. Fires give it off, and decaying matter. And when the chlorophyll combines carbon dioxide with water the plant gives back oxygen, which we need. The whole process of the chlorophyll combining water and carbon dioxide to make sugar and starches and to give back oxygen is called *photosynthesis*, which means *putting things together with light*."

"The sun is a plant's best friend," Bill said with a chuckle.

"One of them," Uncle John corrected. "The soil is another."

## Understanding the Soil

Uncle John leaned down and scooped up a handful of dirt. "It takes about six hundred years," he said, "to make an inch of topsoil like that."

"How is it made?"

"By breaking up rock," Uncle John answered. "The air helps, for the oxygen in the air mixes with chemicals in the rock and makes it decay. Water, too—the rain, the snow—break up rock. And glaciers and rivers and the wind carry topsoil from one area and deposit it on the rock of another area. The roots of plants also break up the earth. A tiny root hair can split a rock!

"In the 1700's when this country was still largely a wilderness," Uncle John said, "the average topsoil was about nine inches deep."

"Just a minute," Bill interrupted. "Nine inches times six hundred years means that nature took forty-five hundred years to build up that topsoil."

"Right," Uncle John agreed. "But now in the 1900's the topsoil averages only six inches, so that in two hundred years man has used up what it took nature eighteen hundred years to build."

Bill frowned. "Gee, if we go on at that rate, we'll get into serious trouble!"

"In some parts of the country we're already in trouble," Uncle John said. "But science is helping us. Unlike the Mayans, we can't move on and build new cities when the soil wears out. We must learn that if we cut down too many trees we leave the soil so loose that the rain carries it away. We must learn that if we keep planting a crop like wheat year after year, we loosen the ground and the wind will blow the loose topsoil away. We must learn that if cattle and sheep graze too long on the same field, they destroy too much of its protective grasses."

"How can we stop such awful things?" Bill demanded.

"One way," Uncle John said, "is to plant rows of trees to shelter fields from the wind. Another is to rotate crops and give the fields a covering of grasses that will keep the rain from washing away the soil. Another is by *contour plowing* across the slope of the land so that the rain water finds it harder to run off the field.

"And, of course," Uncle John continued, "scientists work not only to save the soil, but to keep it healthy. All living things must have cer-

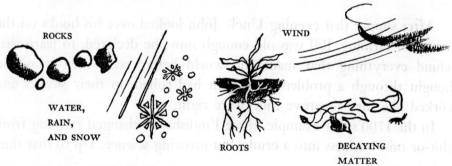

ROCKS      WIND

WATER, RAIN, AND SNOW    ROOTS    DECAYING MATTER

ALL THESE THINGS HELP MAKE TOPSOIL

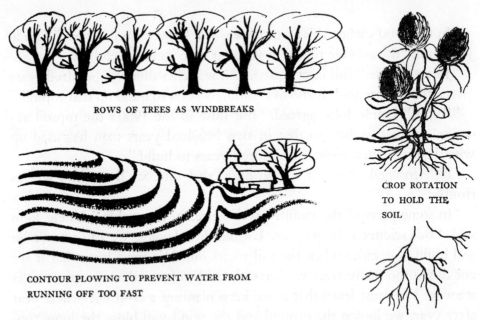

ROWS OF TREES AS WINDBREAKS

CROP ROTATION
TO HOLD THE
SOIL

CONTOUR PLOWING TO PREVENT WATER FROM
RUNNING OFF TOO FAST

ALL THESE THINGS HELP SAVE TOPSOIL

tain chemicals in their food, such as nitrogen, sodium, potassium, calcium, phosphorus, magnesium, iron, and chlorines. When plants use up too much of these essential substances in the soil, we have to put them back. That's what fertilizers are for."

"A farmer's work is never done," Bill grumbled.

Uncle John laughed. "In spite of all the problems a farmer has today, life on the farm is a lot easier and better than it used to be."

## Some Great Men of Agriculture

After supper that evening Uncle John looked over his books on the history of farming. Bill was old enough now, he declared, to learn that behind everything that made the world better were men who had thought through a problem, and then had rolled up their sleeves and worked like fury to prove they were right.

In the 1700's, for example, three Englishmen changed farming from a hit-or-miss business into a crude, but growing science. Up to that time farmers had scattered seeds on the ground, covered them over, and waited for them to come up where they would. But now Jethro Tull invented a drill so that seeds could be dropped in a row, and he even invented a horse-drawn cultivator that helped break up the soil. Then a large landowner, Viscount Townshend, showed his neighbors another new wrinkle. By planting wheat, turnips, barley, and clover over four successive years, he was the first to demonstrate how crop rotation kept the soil healthy. The third Englishman was Robert Blakewell, a sheep raiser, who selected only the best male and female animals to produce flocks superior to those of his neighbors.

And in America, in the 1830's, the farmer found another great friend. His name was Cyrus Hall McCormick. To understand how great McCormick's contribution was to the future of farming, Uncle John said, Bill should think of what it meant to cut a field of grain with a hand sickle. A good farmer—if his back didn't break—could cut an acre a day. McCormick's father, who was also an inventor, worked for years to build a machine that would do this work. His son, Cyrus, kept at the problem, and at the age of twenty-two found the answer!

McCormick's first reaper was a horse-drawn machine with a cutting bar set between two wheels. Triangular knives, guided by steel guards, slid forward and back on the bar. A reel bent the grain so that it could be cut. It was then laid on a platform and a man, following the machine, raked it into piles.

"You wait until harvesting time comes," Uncle John told Bill. "Wait till you see how the modern, tractor-drawn harvester works. It rakes up its own grain, bundles it, ties it with twine. You can harvest from ten to fifteen acres a day with that reaper."

"Are both those machines I saw in the barn reapers?" Bill asked.

"No," Uncle John said, "one is a threshing machine, and for that wonder we owe our thanks to two other Americans, John and Hiram Pitts, who invented the first thresher. Come along to the barn," Uncle John urged. "I'll show you something."

What he pointed out to Bill was that the thresher was actually four

A MODERN COMBINE CUTS AND THRESHES THE GRAIN

small machines—a thresher, a separator, a winnowing machine, and a stacker.

"When the grain passes into the thresher," Uncle John explained, "these cylinders with the rows of metal teeth rub the kernels of grain from the straw. Then in the separator this large screen holds back the straw while the grain goes into the winnowing machine where blasts of air blow off the chaff. The clean grain then drops onto this elevator and is carried to the weighing machine, here on the side. Meanwhile the straw travels on this belt from the separator to the stacker where it is blown out onto a haystack."

"You mean all that goes on at once?" Bill demanded.

"That's right!"

"Why, there's nothing to farming any more."

Uncle John cautioned Bill with a farmer's saying: "Don't you go putting the cart before the horse!"

## The Miracle of Hybrid Corn

To give a country enough good food so that its people are healthy, strong, and vigorous isn't something a machine can do. "Men have to do that," Uncle John declared. "By learning about plants, and finding methods to help plants grow better." A food America had given to the world—corn—could tell a dramatic story of how science had improved the quality of the food.

Corn had been growing in America when the white man landed here. Sailors, exploring this new world, reported to Columbus that they had discovered "a sort of grain" called maize, and the Indians had taught the Pilgrims how to raise corn. If Bill flew in an airplane from ocean to ocean, or from our northern border to the Rio Grande, he would look down on a country where more acres were planted in corn than in any other crop.

Yet for a long time—hundreds of years, really—farmers simply let corn grow. "Sometimes the seed from big healthy ears of corn would

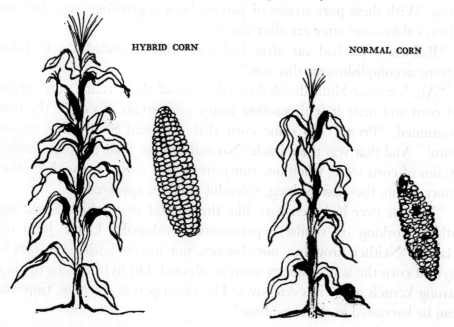

HYBRID CORN                NORMAL CORN

give equally fine corn the next year," Uncle John said, "but sometimes that same seed would produce small, scraggly ears. It was a big gamble, growing corn." Uncle John, chuckling, threw a question at Bill: "To produce a child, what do you have to start with?"

The boy answered with a grin: "A father and mother!"

"And plants also have parents." One scientist who thought about this fact was George H. Shull. The wind, blowing the pollen from the tassels of a corn plant, might carry it to the silk of an ear of corn half an acre away. Thus chance determines the parents of an ear of corn. So Shull decided to control the selection of parents. The method he used was called *inbreeding*, which means that he took the pollen from the tassels and put it on the silk of an ear of corn *on the same plant*. The result was terrible. Never had more sickly corn been produced. Shull continued inbreeding corn this way, and year after year the corn he produced was runty and poor.

"All the children of such parents," Uncle John said, "were the same—miserable runts—and right there Shull grew excited over what he had done. With these pure strains of parents he was growing corn that was always alike—ear after ear after ear."

"Bad ear after bad ear after bad ear," Bill reminded Uncle John. "Some accomplishment, that was!"

"Ah, but now Shull decided to take one of those runty pure strains of corn and mate it with another runty pure strain of corn," the man continued. "Presto! Up came corn that delighted Shull—fine, strong corn!" And that was the miracle. No matter how poor the pure, inbred strains of corn were, when one runty strain was *cross-bred* with another runty strain, these astonishing, splendid children appeared.

"No one ever had seen corn like this *hybrid corn* which Shull, and others working on similar experiments, developed," Uncle John declared. "Neither droughts, nor diseases, nor insects bother the ears of hybrid corn the way ordinary corn is affected. On hybrid corn the big, strong kernels grow in even rows. The ears ripen at the same time and can be harvested at the same time."

But Uncle John admitted there was one joker. The seed of hybrid corn was worthless. Each season new seed had to be secured by crossing pure strains of corn. "Yet," he said, "when you reckon that hybrid corn not only gives you better ears but as much as one-third more corn for every acre, it's worth the trouble."

## A Monk and His Garden

A week later Charley Jones, the county agricultural agent, called at Uncle John's farm. With Charley came old Doc Green, the veterinarian, who wanted to look over Uncle John's cows and chickens to make certain they were free of any disease. Old Doc, squinting a questioning eye at Bill, said: "City kid, I reckon."

"He's learning fast," Uncle John said loyally.

"I can tell you how they developed hybrid corn," Bill said.

Old Doc grunted. "They wouldn't have thought of that, if it hadn't been for a monk named Gregor Johann Mendel. You know about him?"

Bill shook his head.

Old Doc looked pleased as Punch. He liked to tell a story. "At about the time we were fighting the Civil War," he began, "this monk, who lived in Austria, began to wonder about the flowers on the peas in his monastery garden. What Mendel observed was that when he took the male pollen and mated it with the female seed, the new plant shared the characteristics of both parents. When he mated red flowers with white flowers, he got more new plants with red flowers than white flowers, but finally, after much head-scratching, he figured out why.

MENDEL DISCOVERED HOW CHARACTERISTICS ARE PASSED ON

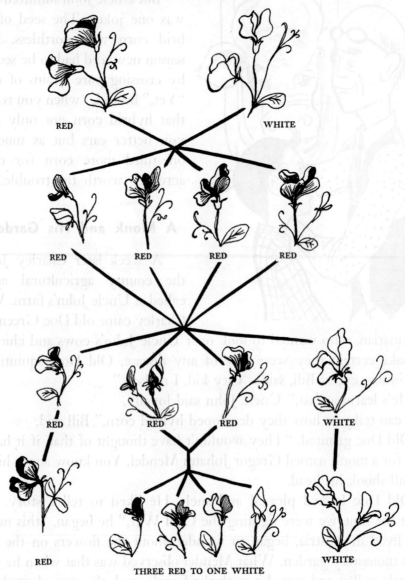

RED          WHITE

RED     RED     RED     RED

RED     RED     RED     WHITE

RED

RED          WHITE

THREE RED TO ONE WHITE

"What Mendel decided," old Doc said, "was that both the male pollen and the female seed possessed atoms, or *genes*, which transferred the characteristics of the parents to the new plant. He decided, too, that some genes were stronger or more dominant than other genes. For example, the red gene dominated the white gene and that was why he got more red flowers than white flowers on his peas."

"You mean," Bill said, "it's like a dog having two or three black pups and only one white pup, because the black genes dominate?"

"Exactly. Genes determine the characteristics not only of plants, but also of all animals—including you and me. If you're more like one parent than the other in the color of your eyes, or the shape of your face, then you can tell whose genes dominated in passing on that characteristic." Old Doc grinned at Bill's astonishment. Folk always seemed surprised to find out about those tricky genes.

"Mendel published a paper about his theory the year after our Civil War ended," Doc said, "but it was not until more than thirty years later —in 1910—that scientists paid serious attention to *Mendel's law of heredity*.

"It wasn't long after that," old Doc went on, "that Shull started the experiments that led to hybrid corn. Everything we do now in producing pure-bred plants and animals is based on the monk's discovery. We try to match up the best characteristics in the parents so that the good traits of both will dominate. That's what *pure breeding* really is!"

"Gee," Bill said, "a fellow in the city sits down to dinner and the fine vegetables or the juicy steak he eats he takes for granted. He thinks it just happens that way!"

"Well, it doesn't," old Doc snorted. "Not in a month of Sundays!"

## A Healthy Nation Is No Accident

Before the summer ended, Bill learned how truthfully old Doc had spoken. Every three or four weeks Charley Jones, the county agricultural agent, appeared at Uncle John's farm. He was a human hawk, that Charley, looking for bugs that might attack the wheat or corn. And Charley always knew the sprays to use to get rid of corn-borers or wheat weevils or caterpillars on the leaves of tomatoes. And Charley dug up

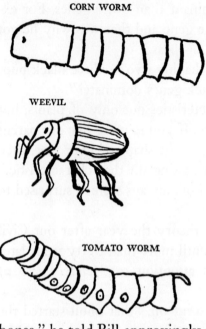

CORN WORM

WEEVIL

TOMATO WORM

samples of soil and sent them to the State College of Agriculture where scientists tested them and decided what kind of fertilizers to use to keep the land healthy and productive.

"You know under what President the United States Department of Agriculture was started?" Charley asked Bill one day.

"No," Bill replied.

"Under Abe Lincoln," Charley said. "He called it 'the people's department' and it sure is!"

Old Doc Green was another regular visitor to the farm. "You're putting more flesh on those city bones," he told Bill approvingly.

"Uncle John feeds me like a horse," Bill answered.

"Health is no accident," old Doc declared. "Good food builds strength and energy. You can't build up flesh and blood without protein, and you can get protein only from plants, or from an animal that has eaten plants. There's a good reason why we use the old Greek word *protein*. It means *I am first*, and sure enough, protein is if you want to lick your weight in wildcats."

Old Doc was off on one of his spiels. He couldn't be stopped. "Wouldn't we be a sorry lot," he demanded, "without body-building foods like vegetables, fruit, eggs, cheese, and milk? They give us the minerals, calcium, and phosphorus without which our bones and teeth wouldn't be any better than matchsticks. They give us the iron necessary for healthy blood. They give us the vitamins that fill us full of pep.

"A boy's a fool if he doesn't eat what he should," old Doc growled. "Science has found out what his body needs. Fellows like your Uncle John, with help from Charley Jones and an old grouch like me, can raise the best food in the world. We've got the machines to harvest it, too —as much as the whole nation can eat!"

Old Doc scowled at Bill, as though he'd take him across his knee and whale the daylights out of him, if he didn't eat properly. The boy grinned.

Uncle John's letters to Bill's parents, telling how Bill was putting on weight and learning the science of good farming, brought an unexpected reward.

"When you return home," Father wrote Bill, "take the train to Central City; then fly the rest of the way."

His first flight! Bill read the letter again, to make sure he was right. Then he shouted: "Hot diggity!"

## 5 The WONDERFUL WHEEL: From Ox Cart to Jet Planes

FROM Uncle John's farm a narrow dirt road twisted through the woods. Some called it the Old Indian Trail, some the Plank Road. Bill loved the road. It was quiet and private and gave a fellow a chance to think. The day before he was to leave for home, Bill shuffled along the road, sure no other person was within miles of him, when a familiar voice called:

"You'll need a bath tonight to get rid of this dust!"

From among the trees stepped Charley Jones, the county agent. Charley had been marking old trees to cut down and deciding where to plant new trees. Bill thought, "Fellows like Uncle John and Charley deserve their success at farming." They knew how important this belt of timber was in sheltering the topsoil. They cared for these trees. But Charley's thoughts were on Bill's journey the next day. Resting a hand on the fallen trunk of an oak, Charley asked:

"Cut off the end of this trunk about two inches thick and what would you have?"

"A piece of trunk about two inches thick," Bill responded brightly.

"You'd have a wheel!" Charley said. "You'd have one of the greatest things man ever discovered! Why, finding how to make a wheel was like solving the secret of electricity or heat or how to grow things!"

Charley sat on the trunk of the old oak and lit his corncob pipe. "From ox cart to jet planes," Charley said, "man could move anywhere, once he knew how to use a wheel."

"I reckon today you'll find more jet planes than ox carts," Bill declared.

"Maybe so," Charley answered. He wasn't sure. "People still use primitive methods for moving around on wheels. Oxen are employed in parts of Africa, and dogs in Belgium and Holland, and camels in India, and water buffalo in Ceylon, and in Japan jinrikishas are drawn by manpower," he said. Bill could still find horses and mules pulling wagons right here in the United States, if he knew where to look, even though

PEOPLE USED PRIMITIVE METHODS FOR MOVING AROUND ON WHEELS

that was hard to believe when you sped along a modern highway in an automobile.

## All About Roads

Charley laughed. "Some difference between this road that, Indian-fashion, follows the course of least resistance by going around obstacles, and a modern highway that tunnels through mountains or spans bays and rivers with great bridges."

"Why do they call it old Plank Road?" Bill asked.

"Go down three miles from here," Charley replied, "and you'll find the remains of logs that were used on this road more than fifty years ago. Such roads also were called *corduroy roads*. By placing logs side by side you built a solid surface so that after a heavy rain you weren't stuck in the mud every few yards."

Charley knew all about roads. The first good road-builders were the ancient Romans, who made their roads higher in the middle—or gave

SOME ANCIENT ROMAN ROADS ARE STILL USED TODAY. THEY WERE MADE OF STONE, AND CONSTRUCTED SO THE WATER WOULD DRAIN OFF

them a *crown*—so that water drained into ditches along the sides. Most early roads in America were much like this old Plank Road—no more than overgrown Indian trails. After a long, heavy rain a horse might sink in mud up to its belly. Charley grinned.

"Some farmers kept mud holes in the road deliberately," he said. "They wanted a coach to get stuck. Then they hitched up their oxen and, for a price, pulled out the luckless travelers."

"What a mean trick!" Bill declared.

Charley wouldn't deny it. But that wasn't his point. *What* was moving on wheels decided the kind of road you built. For stagecoaches, corduroy roads were fine. "You might bounce like a pill in a box," Charley admitted, "but you got where you were going." Later—along about 1900 —roads seemed less important than before, except in cities, for trains had become the chief means of transportation, and roads were planned simply to bounce you to the rail center where you caught the train and traveled on rails. But then along came the automobile, and Americans grew sick of mud and remembered a chap named John L. McAdam. "Say the last name fast," Charley suggested.

Bill repeated: "McAdam—macadam!"

"That's the idea," Charley said. "McAdam was a Scot who, along about 1815, hit upon the fact that when limestone is moistened and crushed down, it provides a hard, smooth surface. So the *macadam road* came into being, and later hot asphalt was used to bind the limestone rocks together. Other materials also were tried in building better roads —cobblestones, bricks, square blocks of granite, even wooden blocks held together by tar. Today concrete is a principal surfacing for roads. A lot of crushed stone also is used."

## A Modern Paul Bunyan

Charley said that nothing gave him a bigger kick than riding along a modern highway. He took his hat off to highway engineers. And the bridge-builders—now there, in Charley's opinion, were a real breed of men. They were the modern Paul Bunyans, stretching great suspension bridges like the Golden Gate Bridge across San Francisco Bay or the George Washington Memorial Bridge across the Hudson River between New York and New Jersey. Or they built a wonderful cantilever bridge like the Huey P. Long Bridge across the Mississippi River at New Orleans—and that was 3,254 feet of bridge, if Bill wanted an exact figure.

"Suspension bridge, cantilever bridge," Bill complained. "You're clear as mud to me."

Charley chuckled. "A *suspension bridge*," he explained, "is one hung on cables fastened to towers on each bank. A *cantilever bridge* is usually built in two sections, sometimes called *arms*. These sections are supported on piers and extended from opposite banks. The arms meet above the middle of a stream."

Among early American bridge-builders, Charley thought, three deserved to be remembered. One was James Buchanan Eads, who built the fleet of gunboats that helped the Yankees win the Civil War along the Mississippi River, and who in 1874 built a great steel arch bridge over the same river between St. Louis, Missouri, and East St. Louis, Illinois. Four piers, resting on the bedrock far beneath the mud of the Mississippi, supported the Eads Bridge.

"What do you mean, an *arch bridge?*" Bill demanded.

Charley said that he wasn't trying to confuse Bill. The old Romans had built arch bridges. They had wedged stone blocks against each other, with the stone at the top called the *keystone*. When a weight is placed on the bridge, the bridge pushes down on the keystone, which pushes down on the blocks next to it, and so the weight is passed on from block to block until it reaches the bottom of the arch.

"And that holds it up?"

Charley nodded.

Bill looked suspicious. "You got any other kinds of bridges to spring on me?"

Charley grinned. "Well, there's the *trestle bridge*, which trains run over. And the simple *beam bridge*, which you can make by putting a

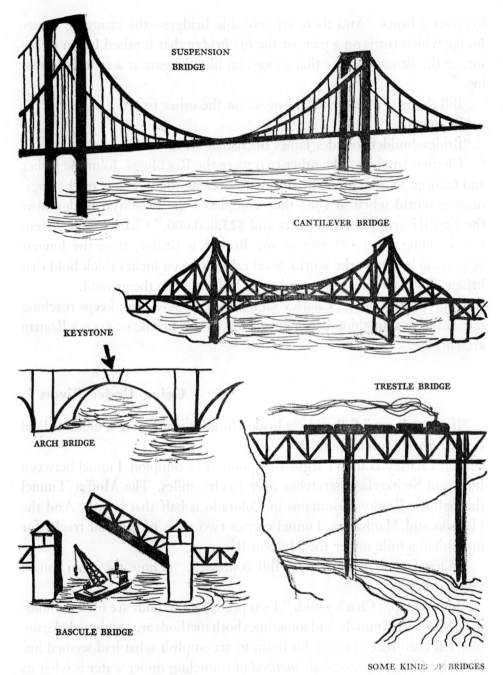

SUSPENSION BRIDGE

CANTILEVER BRIDGE

KEYSTONE

ARCH BRIDGE

TRESTLE BRIDGE

BASCULE BRIDGE

SOME KINDS OF BRIDGES

log over a brook. And there are movable bridges—the *swinging draw-bridge* which turns on a pier, or the *lift bridge* that is raised by an elevator, or the *bascule bridge* that swings up like the gate at a railroad crossing."

Bill thought a moment. "How about the other two?"

"Two what?"

"Bridge-builders besides James Buchanan Eads."

Charley laughed. The other two were the Roeblings, John the father and George Washington the son, who became the wonders of the engineering world when in 1883 they completed the Brooklyn Bridge over the East River. "Fourteen years and $25,000,000," Charley said, "went into building the 1,595 feet of the Brooklyn Bridge, then the longest suspension bridge in the world. Steel cables sixteen inches thick hold that bridge. The towers at either end rise 275 feet above the ground.

"It gives me a boot," Charley said, "thinking how man keeps reaching out, wanting something better than a log over a brook, or even a Roman arch bridge."

### Going Under Rivers

"If you ask me," Bill said, "a bridge-builder is no more a modern Paul Bunyan than a tunnel-builder."

But Charley couldn't argue that point. The Simplon Tunnel between Italy and Switzerland stretches over twelve miles. The Moffat Tunnel through the Rocky Mountains in Colorado is half that length. And the Hudson and Manhattan Tunnel carries two pairs of railroad tracks for more than a mile under the Hudson River.

"What I don't understand," Bill confessed, "is how they can tunnel under water."

"It's no snap," Charley said. "Two principal methods are used in building underwater tunnels, and sometimes both methods are employed. Again, man has been forced to use his brain to accomplish what had seemed impossible. The *compressed-air method* of tunneling under water is what its

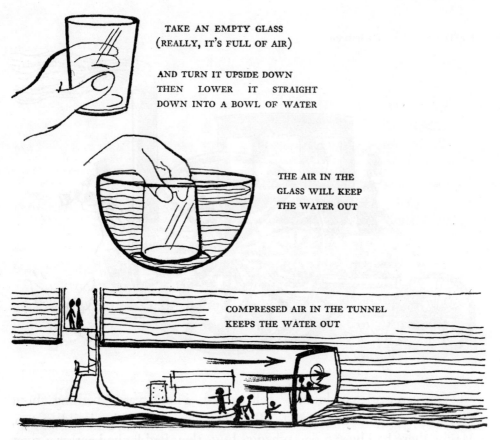

TAKE AN EMPTY GLASS
(REALLY, IT'S FULL OF AIR)

AND TURN IT UPSIDE DOWN
THEN LOWER IT STRAIGHT
DOWN INTO A BOWL OF WATER

THE AIR IN THE
GLASS WILL KEEP
THE WATER OUT

COMPRESSED AIR IN THE TUNNEL
KEEPS THE WATER OUT

YOU CAN SEE FOR YOURSELF THAT AIR KEEPS WATER OUT

name suggests—by compressing the air in the end of the tunnel where the men are working, the pressure of the in-coming water is held back.

"In the *shield system,* a cylinder of steel plate is used. The front of the cylinder is sharply pointed. On the inside of the cylinder are jacks operated by water pressure. The jacks push the lining of the finished tunnel tight while the cutting edge of the shield shoves ahead. If the earth in the river bed is soft, the shield simply pushes it aside. But small vents in the shield can be opened to let the earth pass through, if you have to get it out that way. Section by section the cast-iron lining of a tunnel is bolted into place.

"It takes courage to build," Charley said.

TREVITHICK'S STEAM CARRIAGE

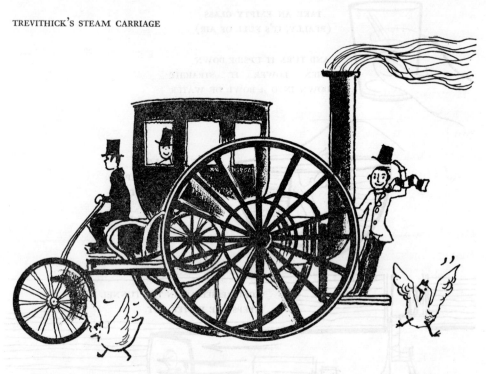

"You can say that double," Bill agreed. There was something about those tunnel-builders that excited Bill. And about the bridge-builders, too. Maybe there had been a day when as boys they had looked across a river or bay and thought, "There's an easier way to get across that!" A dream then—and now a fact! "Gee!" Bill muttered, for a reason Charley did not quite understand.

## From Steamers to Gasoline

Next morning Uncle John drove Bill to the railroad station.

"Never did really like these infernal automobiles," Uncle John growled. "I was about your age when cars began to become popular. Wasn't a horse for miles that wasn't frightened out of its wits!"

Bill grinned. He had been collecting pictures of old automobiles for two years, and now he became the teacher, explaining to Uncle John how, as early as 1769, a French army officer, Nicholas Joseph Cugnot, had invented a steam-driven tractor to haul artillery weapons. Cugnot's steamer could get up to three miles an hour—when it wasn't broken down—but one day it upset going around a corner and was barred from the roads. About 1800 in England the first steam-propelled carriage, the invention of Richard Trevithick, appeared. "He could manage up to ten miles an hour," Bill said, chuckling, "which is faster than a chicken can go down a road!"

"They were deliberate rascals and chicken-chasers, those early drivers!" Uncle John declared with a snort.

"More than likely," Bill admitted. "The first horseless buggy in America," he said, "was built in Springfield, Massachusetts in 1893 by Charles and J. Franklin Duryea—a classy one-seater driven by chains that connected the engine to the rear wheels. About this time, all over America, other chicken-chasers were being manufactured—by the Apperson brothers and Elwood Haynes in Kokomo, Indiana, by Alexander Winton in Cleveland, Ohio, and by Ransom E. Olds in Lansing, Michigan."

"Henry Ford was the one who raised the big ruckus," Uncle John grumbled.

Bill nodded. "But Ford," he pointed out, "only wanted to take the drudgery out of farming and at first had planned to build a tractor. He had used a kerosene-heated boiler to provide the steam to drive his first vehicle, and had darn near burned a hole in his breeches! The description in a British publication of how to make a small gasoline engine fascinated Ford. He wondered why such an engine couldn't propel a carriage."

## The Menace of Detroit

As early as 1890, Ford began working on a two-cylinder engine that would drive a light flywheel. His first intention was to mount this engine on a bicycle, but when he considered what a mess it would make to load down a bike with a gasoline tank, engine, and various controls,

he knew that notion was impractical. So he built a buggy with a seat suspended on posts and the coach body set on curved springs. His engine had two speeds—one of ten and the other of twenty miles an hour —and by 1896 he was ready to take a spin through the city.

Soon more fists were shaken at Henry Ford than at any other resident of Detroit. His gasoline-driven carriage made a terrible racket. Horses reared up in panic and dumped their buggies. Traffic was snarled. Whenever Ford stopped, crowds swarmed around his curious vehicle, and if he turned his back, someone always tried to run off with his car. "But Ford fooled those early car-thieves," Bill said. "He carried a chain and locked his car to a lamp post whenever he went anywhere!"

"I remember when Ford improved his car and came out with the first Model T," Uncle John said. "That was in 1908. For years that was the only car Ford made—first by the thousands and then by the million till it was taking your life in your hands to walk down a road. Everybody poked fun at that Model T—called it a Flivver and a Tin Lizzie—but they bought 'em. First car I owned was a Model T. You could drive it anywhere—across a ploughed field and almost straight up the side of a barn!"

Even Uncle John admitted that Henry Ford had been a genius. As the demand for automobiles grew, Ford had met that demand by creating the assembly line. A man learned thoroughly one operation in making a car, and as an automobile passed down the line, each man did his own job quicker than it had ever been done before. So Ford changed American business. And American life. Somewhere Uncle John had read that there were 54,000 communities in America that can be reached only by automobile, truck, or bus. Once life in these communities was isolated and lonely. Now the family car takes those people anywhere they wish to go—north, south, east, west.

All at once Uncle John slammed on the brakes. A cow had broken out of its pasture and blocked the road. "Get, *get!*" shouted Uncle John. "Get, you ornery idiot, or I'll make raw meat out of you!"

Tactfully, Bill said nothing. Automobiles had changed Uncle John as well as America.

## Exciting Times in Baltimore

The railroad terminal at Farmville stood at the foot of a mountain range, and steam locomotives were used to haul the freights across the rugged country beyond. What Bill didn't know about Richard Trevithick, whose steam-driven "chicken-chaser" had been the first on the roads of England, was the fact that in 1804 Trevithick had also operated the first steam locomotive to run on rails. Some twenty years later John Stevens, a colonel in the American Revolution, had run a steam locomotive on an experimental track in Hoboken, New Jersey, and in England in 1829 the Stephensons—George the father and Robert the son—had built the famous Rocket, designed along the principles of a modern locomotive, and had seen it zip over the tracks of the Liverpool and Manchester Railway at thirty miles an hour.

In the station at Farmville the calendar by the ticket-window reproduced the picture of still another early steam locomotive—the Tom Thumb.

"Built by Peter Cooper, she was, and run on the tracks of the Baltimore and Ohio," the ticket agent told Bill.

"Can't say she had much of a boiler," Bill commented.

"No bigger than the boiler you'd find in an old kitchen stove," the agent agreed. "Mounted on that small four-wheeled flat car, it's no wonder they named her Tom Thumb."

The agent wasn't busy and as long as Bill would listen he was willing to talk about railroads. "Back in 1829," he said, "when Peter Cooper brought the Tom Thumb to Baltimore, no one had much faith in that peanut gadget. The tracks of the B. & O. in those days ran thirteen miles, between Baltimore and a place called Ellicott's Mills, and there were short curves that the experts believed no steam locomotive could take. So all sorts of other contraptions were tried.

"One was a flat car with a moving platform that a horse trod on," the agent continued. "The platform, pumping up and down, gave the

THE TOM THUMB

power that turned the axles. Well, they tried her, with a lot of dignitaries riding behind in a car with benches, and the poor old horse gave them a pretty good spin until a cow appeared. That cow had fits, rammed engine and car, dumped both down an embankment, and ended the experiment right there. Next they gave Evan Thomas and his Meteor a try. This engine was propelled by a sail, but Thomas had forgotten two facts. For one, the wind didn't always blow when it was most needed. For another, the prevailing wind was eastward and who ever heard of a railroad that ran better in one direction than the other?"

Bill could see this wouldn't work, even if the failure of the Meteor almost broke the heart of Evan Thomas. "On August 28, 1830"—the ticket agent was a crank over small facts—"the Tom Thumb was given her trial on the thirteen-mile run between Baltimore and Ellicott's Mills. They put a small car in front and loaded on twenty-four passengers. Peter Cooper fired his boiler with anthracite coal. In sixty-one minutes the Tom Thumb completed the run, which averaged out to about six miles an hour. Once she stopped four minutes to take in water." The ticket agent forgot nothing.

"And that's the story of the Tom Thumb, the grandpappy of American railroading," he finished triumphantly.

## How Locomotives Operate

Bill thanked the man. A long freight train had pulled into the station to take in water. Bill walked over and the engineer said, "She likes a drink like anybody else on a hot day."

"Without that water to absorb the heat, you wouldn't have steam," Bill said.

Surprised, the engineer looked down. "How do you know that?"

"Our teacher taught us about steam engines—about old Newcomen and his pumping engine and how Watt divided the boiler from the piston-chamber so that he wouldn't waste fuel."

"Well, I'll be jiggered," said the engineer, who broke into a grin so

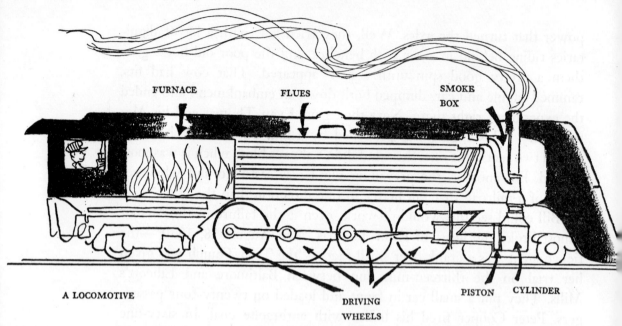

FURNACE     FLUES     SMOKE BOX

A LOCOMOTIVE     DRIVING WHEELS     PISTON    CYLINDER

that being jiggered seemed a pretty good thing to be. "The boiler in a steam locomotive," he explained to Bill, "is a long cylinder of steel with the furnace at one end and the smoke-box at the other. You can burn either coal or fuel oil, and the tubes that carry the smoke and gas through the cylinder are called *flues*. The water they were taking in surrounds the flues and firebox to make the steam, as you know.

"Now," the engineer went on, "that steam enters cylinders on the sides at the front end of the locomotive. Here as the steam expands it forces out pistons that connect to a rod attached to those large wheels here, called *driving wheels*. This side rod carries the force to other wheels. Really a simple gadget, once you understand this big, growlish baby."

"How do you control her?" Bill asked.

"Come along, and I'll let you look in my cab," the engineer offered. Bill nodded eagerly. The man hoisted him up and pointed to the throttle. "That lets the steam into the cylinders by releasing a valve in those domes you see on top of the boiler," he said. "This set of levers reverses the direction of the locomotive, that lever throws on the air brakes, and when I yank this, I drop sand on the tracks."

"You run quite a show up here," Bill said admiringly.

"A railroad man is nobody's stepchild," the engineer answered proudly. Anybody who was good at his work, Bill was learning, liked doing it.

## The Power of 7,000 Horses

"Do you ever run an electric locomotive?" Bill asked.

The engineer nodded. "They have one advantage," he said. "There's no boiler in an electric locomotive. She won't freeze up on you in bitter cold weather. An electric locomotive carries one or two motors hitched by gears to the driving axles, and the beauty is that she's always ready to go, whereas with this baby you don't move till you build up steam. And an electric has power. Run them on overhead wires and you can give them up to 30,000 volts, alternating and direct current. Or run them on a third rail and you use 600 volts. I've seen an electric pull a 5,000-ton freight or twenty-four passenger cars at speeds approaching one hundred miles an hour. Hook together three electrics and you get the driving force of 7,000 horses!"

"Still, for my money," the engineer contended, "no locomotive can beat the diesel-electrics that pull the fast streamliners."

"How are diesels different?" Bill asked.

"Well, I guess you know that in gasoline engines the fuel is ignited by spark. But in a diesel compression of air raises the temperature to the igniting point. Diesels are heavier than gasoline engines, but they use crude oil for fuel, which is cheaper. They're called diesels, by the way, because they were invented by a German engineer, Rudolf Diesel."

"A good diesel-electric will run five hundred miles without needing to fuel up. You hitch them up in sections, and in each unit a sixteen-cylinder, two-cycle diesel engine gives you 1,350-horsepower. With four sections," the engineer said, "you have thirty-two driving wheels. You move."

Down the track the semaphore on the tower moved from a horizontal position to a diagonal position. Its red light on the right blinked off and the yellow light in the center went on.

"Is that for you?" Bill inquired.

"In a railroader's language, it means I can approach. When the semaphore moves straight up and the green light glows on the left, then I move so that your train can pull in on this track." The engineer drew four diagrams on a pad:

|  |  |  |  |
|---|---|---|---|
|  |  | 0 |  |
| 000 | 00 | 0 | 0 |
|  |  | 0 |  |
| 1 | 2 | 3 | 4 |

"Those are the signal lights you'll see on this railroad," he told Bill. "When numbers 1 and 2 are set the way I have them here, they mean stop. Set them diagonally, they mean approach. Set them straight, they mean go. Number 3 works from the bottom up—red light for stop, yellow for approach, green for go. On number 4 one light flashes red, yellow, or green."

"Gosh," Bill said, "it sounds simple, but a lot of thinking must have gone into the semaphore system."

SIGNALS MAY BE SEMAPHORE ARMS, POSITION LIGHTS, OR COLORED LIGHTS

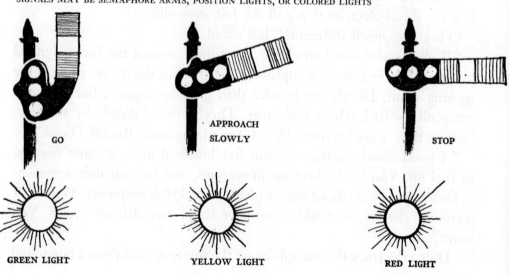

GO

APPROACH
SLOWLY

STOP

GREEN LIGHT

YELLOW LIGHT

RED LIGHT

"Of course it did. Thinking went into building steam locomotives and diesel-electrics, too. Well, my young friend, you'd better get because I've got to pull out."

"Yes, sir!" Bill said. He swung down from the cab. "Thank you, sir— thank you very much!"

The engineer smiled and pulled the throttle. With a long hiss the locomotive started forward.

## Man on the Move

Uncle John got Bill settled in the train, told him to be sure to come back next year, and took his leave.

The run from Farmville to Central City took an hour. Bill watched for the signal lights, but he couldn't fill sixty minutes doing that. "Men thinking," he muttered, "thinking about electricity and heat and wheels and engines." And what had it all meant? Suddenly Bill found himself playing Miss Pringle's game, "You Name It."

How had man learned to move? By foot first—a slow, tiresome way to travel. And by boat and sled. Or on the backs of animals—horses on firm land, camels in the desert. And then in carts on wheels pulled by animals, and finally by engines and motors doing the driving so that, as the engineer had said, a four-section diesel-electric locomotive could do the job of 7,000 horses. Over rivers or under them, over mountains or through them—man kept moving, a pioneer at heart seeking frontiers to a better life and using his brain to find and conquer those frontiers.

"It gives me goose-pimples," Bill said to himself. In his mind he saw a long procession of people marching—the cavemen, the first farmers, knights in armor riding off to the crusades, American frontiersmen in their buckskins, Peter Cooper aboard Tom Thumb, Henry Ford bouncing along in a horseless buggy.

Outside the train window the passing countryside gave way to the factories and rows of houses that announced the approach of a city. Overhead the sun shone brilliantly in a cloudless sky. The sky! Bill gulped. Soon that's where he'd be—soaring across that sky!

### 6. The SKY ABOVE: Man Imitates the Flight of Birds

THE busiest place Bill had ever seen was the airlines terminal at Central City. Loudspeakers blared constantly:

"Flight 62 to St. Louis is now ready for departure from Gate 12 on the west ramp . . . Flight 123, nonstop from New York, is arriving at East Gate 7 . . . Bad weather has delayed the arrival of Flight 38 approximately forty-five minutes . . ."

Passengers milled around Bill like cattle in a stockyard. Then he realized that Flight 38 was *his* plane. Bewildered by the terminal's bustle, Bill wandered back to the waiting room. He was lucky to find a seat. A man whose thin body and head resembled a stovepipe with a knob on it spoke sympathetically.

"Is that delayed flight yours?"

"Yes, sir."

"It's mine, too. This your first flight?"

"Do I look that much like a greenhorn?"

The man chuckled. "I've been flying for years. I can tell. My name's Smith. I design airplanes."

"Mr. Smith," Bill said, "I hope you design good planes that stay up in the air."

"Indeed I do," Mr. Smith assured Bill with a grin. "The air helps, of course. How much do you know about air?"

"Just that I breathe it in," Bill answered.

## What the Air Is

Bill didn't need to apologize for that fact, Mr. Smith said. Most people know very little about air, although without it nobody could live more than a few minutes. People know vaguely that air is a mixture of gases, and perhaps even that oxygen and nitrogen make up about 99 per cent of the air. And the other 1 per cent? That is a gas called argon mostly, *plus* carbon dioxide, hydrogen, neon, helium, krypton, and ozone, *plus* salt particles from the sea and dust particles from the earth, *plus* microbes, *plus* grains of pollen and the spores from plants.

"The trouble with air," Mr. Smith said, "is that you can't see it because it is colorless. You can't taste it or smell it. Yet air

MR. SMITH WROTE A FIGURE

is as much a substance as water. It can be weighed." Mr. Smith wrote a figure on the margin of his newspaper: 6,000,000,000,000,000. Then he added the word "tons."

"Six million billion tons," he said. "That's the total weight of the air around the earth. The pressure of air at sea level is fifteen pounds to every square inch of the earth's surface."

"You'd think we'd all be flattened like pancakes," Bill remarked.

"Well, we aren't. Nature adapts our bodies to this pressure—but when you design an airplane you have to remember what air is. You remember that any object moving through air must meet with resistance—and the faster an object travels, the more resistance it meets."

"Then how," Bill demanded, "can an airplane force its way through the air?"

"It doesn't. It *slips* through." Mr. Smith pointed to the pictures around the waiting room. "Those murals tell the story of how man learned to fly. Let me explain them to you."

## Icarus Melts His Wings

Watching birds soaring overhead, man yearned to fly. The fact that nothing happened when he flapped his arms didn't destroy the yearning. His legends were filled with heroes born of the wish to fly. In Egypt the sun-god became a flying falcon. The Greeks gave winged heels to the god Hermes and the Norse sent their men of legend through space on winged horses.

"This first picture," Mr. Smith told Bill, "relates the legend of Daedalus and Icarus, who lived on the island of Crete where they were imprisoned by King Minos. Daedalus told his son Icarus: 'Minos may control the land and sea, but not the regions of the air.' So he fashioned wings of feathers fastened with thread and wax and warned Icarus: 'If you fly too high, the heat of the sun will melt the wax.' Away the pair soared. Icarus, thrilled by heights, flew up, up, up until he could no

ICARUS FLEW UP, UP, UP . . .

longer hear the frantic cries of his father. Alas, the sun melted his wax wings. He plunged to his death in the sea."

"Why couldn't primitive man see that he wasn't made like a bird?" Bill asked critically.

"In many details the structure of your arm *is* like the wing of a bird."

"I still can't fly," said a practical Bill, and Mr. Smith couldn't dispute this assertion. Still, other murals on the wall proved that for centuries man clung to the notion that by attaching wings to himself he could fly. Was it all legend that four hundred years before Christ a Greek, Archytas, built a wooden bird powered by gas that actually flew? Leonardo da Vinci, whose portrait of Mona Lisa is one of the most famous paintings in the world, designed a two-part flapping wing and invented, as far as we know, the parachute and the propeller.

### From Besner to the Wrights

"Look there," Mr. Smith said. "That's Besner, a French locksmith, who, in 1670, attached paddlelike cloth wings to his shoulders and feet and jumped from a high window. Moving his wings as a bird would in flight, he glided to the ground. After that the possibility of flying by glider or other mechanical means fascinated many, among them Otto Lilienthal in Germany. He had watched storks and patterned his glider so that his body dangled beneath broad wings. He balanced himself by swinging his legs. Lilienthal flew for distances up to one thousand feet and made about two thousand flights before an old, shaky wing collapsed and killed him.

"Even fatal disasters didn't discourage the early pioneers of aviation. In America Octave Chanute built an excellent biplane glider, and a Californian, John J. Montgomery, discovered that a curved wing surface gave him a better glider. Working with Montgomery was a parachute jumper named Maloney, a daredevil who used a hot-air balloon to raise the glider so that he could cut loose and sweep down, curving and dipping, from altitudes of three and four thousand feet."

"It's a wonder any of them lived," Bill declared.

Mr. Smith nodded. "Meanwhile," he said, "another group of pioneers had sprung up who believed that airplane flight depended upon the use of power. One of the earliest experimenters was William Samuel Henson, an Englishman who, about 1842, patented a model of a steam-propelled plane called the Ariel. People scoffed at Henson and no one would back him financially. Yet six years later a co-worker, John Stringfellow, constructed a model airplane that did fly 120 feet. Another English experimenter was Sir Hiram Maxim who built a plane that weighed over five thousand pounds. A steam engine drove two propellers and there was only one thing wrong with that plane—it wouldn't fly.

"In France," Mr. Smith continued, "Clement Ader came forward in the late 1890's with the Avion. This plane was shaped like a bird and two

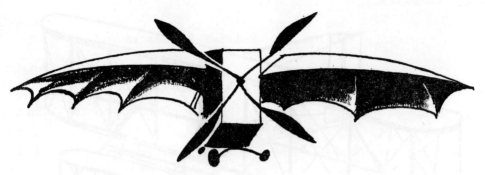

ADER'S "AVION" LOOKED LIKE A BIRD

steam engines, each of twenty-horsepower, turned feather-like propellers. The closest the Avion came to flying was a few little hops."

"You'd think they'd all quit after a time," Bill said.

"Would *you*, if you really believed in an idea?"

"Well—" Bill paused. What could you gain by quitting? Suppose Shull had quit on hybrid corn or Edison on the light bulb or Ford on the horseless buggy? "No, I wouldn't," he said. "I reckon the only way an inventor can stand being laughed at is by knowing in his heart he's going to have the last laugh!"

## Triumph at Kitty Hawk

"Right you are," Mr. Smith agreed. "And even failure can have odd results. Reading about the death of Otto Lilienthal in Germany, a chap in Dayton, Ohio, grew interested in aviation. His name was Wilbur Wright, and with his brother Orville he ran a bicycle repair shop. 'I am an enthusiast, but not a crank,' Wilbur told officials at the Smithsonian Institution in 1899 when he wrote for literature on flying. In the next few years Will and Orv experimented with gliders, constructed gasoline engines, built a wind tunnel for testing wing strain. Sister Katherine sewed covering for wings while her brothers read themselves half blind mastering subjects like geography and weather.

" 'Those sand dunes around Kitty Hawk, North Carolina, seem the best place to test our plane,' Wilbur decided at last.

THE WRIGHT BROTHERS' FIRST SUCCESSFUL PLANE

"The year was 1903. That October people laughed over 'Langley's folly!' The butt of their ridicule was Samuel Pierpont Langley, who had been experimenting with planes for seventeen years. Now Langley had completed a plane weighing 730 pounds, driven by a gasoline engine. A small model had flown successfully, so Langley felt he was ready to launch his airship from a houseboat on the Potomac River. He tried twice—on October 7th and December 8th—and both times his plane plunged into the river.

"The Wright brothers were at Kitty Hawk all this time, trying to work out the 'bugs' in their own craft. First, the hollow-tube shafts of the propellers buckled. Then two sprockets worked loose on the chain drive from the engine to the propellers. Then a gale blew for a week and the shafts broke again. This time they built shafts of solid steel. By December 17th they were ready to launch the plane down the glide track they had constructed.

"A wind blew from the north, somewhere between twenty and twenty-five miles an hour. Five people—including a 16-year-old boy and three men from the nearby life-saving station—were the only witnesses. Engine and propellers were worked out; then at 10:35 A.M. Orv 'got on the machine.' The rope was slipped off. Down the track glided the plane, picking up speed to seven miles an hour—eight—perhaps nine—and up into the air it lifted for about twelve seconds! The second trial was no better, and on the third Orv wobbled up to twelve or fourteen feet when a bad gust of wind brought him down. Once more the plane was carried back, set on her track, the rope slipped off. This time Orv stayed aloft for fifty-nine seconds, flying over a ground distance of 852 feet!

"None of the five spectators at Kitty Hawk realized that they had witnessed the birth of the air age," Mr. Smith said. "But all these other murals followed because the Wrights succeeded. Man could do it—he could fly like a bird—but in time higher, faster!"

## Why a Plane Flies

Bill had forgotten about the time. Like a thunderclap, the loudspeakers announced: "Passengers for Flight 38. Your plane will be landing at East Gate 16 in approximately ten minutes."

"Let's watch it," Mr. Smith said. "Landing a plane is quite an art."

When they reached the observation deck, they still could not see their plane approaching, but Mr. Smith pointed to a big four-engine plane waiting to receive passengers and said, "That's like ours. Four things are involved in flying a plane. First is *gravity*—the downward pull of the earth—which keeps everything, including you and me, from flying into space. A plane overcomes that pull with an opposite force called *lift*, which is created by the motion of air over and under its wings."

"Explain, please," said Bill with a grin.

"When flying a kite," Mr. Smith replied, "why do you tilt the kite to raise it in the air?" He went on, without giving Bill a chance to answer, which he couldn't have done, anyway. "First, air puts pressure on whatever it strikes. Second, when air strikes a tilted surface (like a kite or a wing), part of the force tends to lift that surface. And a discovery made in Switzerland some two hundred years ago by a mathematician, Jakob

Bernoulli, also is involved. The pressure of a gas, Bernoulli found, became less as the speed of a gas increased. Therefore, as the speed decreased, the pressure increased.

"Now apply these rules to air, which is a mixture of gases, and to a tilted wing," Mr. Smith continued. "When the air strikes the tilted wing, its speed is greater above than below."

"Why is the speed greater?"

"Because we curve the top of the wing, giving the air less resistance. Below the wing, the air hits a flat surface and exerts greater pressure. A good engineer does more than curve his wing to produce lift. He makes his front edges thicker than the back edges. He understands that the pressure of the air under the wing, which he calls *drag*, helps only if the wing is tilted at the proper angle. And he has a term for that— the *angle of attack*."

"As though he were at war with gravity?"

"In a way."

"What would happen," Bill asked, "if the tilt was too much?"

"The air would swirl around on top of the wing and the balance of lift and drag would be lost so that the plane would 'stall'—or fall to the ground.

"So you see that a wing has two jobs to do. It must increase the lift. And, as much as possible, it must decrease the drag. We try all kinds of tricks in design," Mr. Smith said, "to lessen the drag. For one, we eliminate the rivets with a special kind of welding. For another, we round the front of the wing and make the rear long and tapering—or *stream-line* it."

"Still," Bill insisted, "you have to get the plane off the ground."

"With what we call *thrust*," Mr. Smith explained. "The propeller blades supply that force. Those blades are really small wings. They, too, have lift and drag. And what they do actually is to pull the plane through the air. In short, the propeller cuts down the air pressure in front of the spinning blades.

"There are three ways," the designer said, "that a pilot manages his

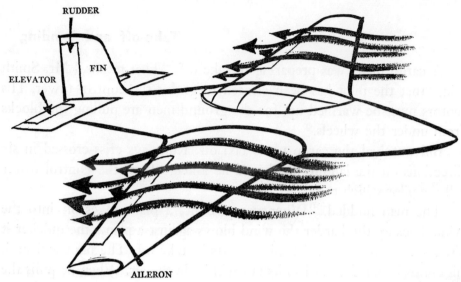

RUDDER

FIN

ELEVATOR

AILERON

BECAUSE AIR HAS TO FLOW FASTER OVER THE TOP OF THE WING, THERE IS LESS PRESSURE THERE THAN ON THE FLAT UNDERSURFACE

plane to help it fly. Hinged flaps (*ailerons*) can be moved up and down on the sides of the wings. This is called *rolling*. By controlling the tail of his plane (called the *stabilizer*, which is like a wing and one-ninth its size with flaps attached to the rear) he can *pitch*—that is, thrust the nose of the plane suddenly downward or upward. Or by using the rudder on the tail fin he can *yaw*—that is, swing the nose from side to side.

"Bend the flaps on the stabilizer down," Mr. Smith said, "and the plane dives. Turn them up, and the plane climbs. The rudder turns the plane right and left, and for sharp turns—called *banking*—the side flaps (ailerons) are set one up and one down."

A plane designer has another problem to consider. The exterior hull of his plane—that is, the covering of the part where crew, passengers and baggage are carried—is called the *fuselage*. The normal tendency of a propeller would be to rotate the fuselage in a direction opposite to the motion of the propeller. "But we get around that," Mr. Smith said. "Sometimes two propellers turn in opposite directions and so balance out. Or one wing may be larger than the other, or one may have a greater angle of attack than the other."

### Take-off and Landing

A cargo plane was preparing to take off. "That means," Mr. Smith said, "that the pilot has been cleared to go by the control tower. His motors must be warmed up, for the ground men are pulling the blocks from under the wheels."

Bill watched the cargo plane taxi off. Runways criss-crossed in six directions on the landing field, and he asked, "Does the control tower tell the pilot which to take?"

The man nodded. "Whenever possible, a plane takes off into the wind, because the harder the wind blows against a plane, the quicker it rises. You watch when that plane starts its take-off. The pilot will push his control stick forward so its tail will be in the air. When he pulls the stick back, the plane rises. After the plane is off the ground, the pilot lets it level off to gain speed before he starts to climb to his cruising altitude."

With a roar, the cargo plane started and took off. Then overhead Bill heard the drone of a four-engine transport and guessed, "That's our plane."

"She's come over five hundred miles on this hop, and probably she's come most of the way without seeing the ground," Mr. Smith said.

"How do they know where they're going?"

"They fly by radio beacons that send out two letters in Morse code—an N (dash dot) and an A (dot dash). When the plane is on course the two signals blend into a continuous da sound (dash), but should the

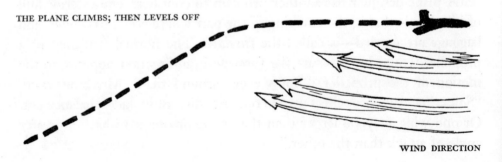

THE PLANE CLIMBS; THEN LEVELS OFF

WIND DIRECTION

pilot get off course, either the N or A signal will tell him the direction of his proper flying beam."

"That's a system!" Bill exclaimed.

Mr. Smith smiled. "Radio beacons enable a plane to land even when the pilot can't see the field. Usually the landing descent starts about three miles from the end of the runway, and in landing the pilot brings his craft into the wind so that his wings will have their fullest lift. First, the motors are slowed down and the propellers pull the plane at low speed. Next, the stick is shoved forward and the plane nosed down. A few feet above the ground the pilot levels off and finally raises the nose. The air flow over the wings is cut off. The wings 'stall.' In a perfect *three-point landing* the two front wheels and the tail wheel touch the ground at the same time."

The pilot of the plane on Flight 38 landed just as the designer predicted.

## Bill's Flying Horses

When Bill boarded the plane, a lighted sign at the front of the passenger cabin read: FASTEN SEAT BELTS. The boy asked: "Do they expect trouble?"

"No," Mr. Smith answered. "At take-off and landing you strap yourself as a safety precaution against a sudden sideward movement or bounce. Otherwise you can move around as you like unless you hit a bad piece of air or weather. There are updrafts when the air is warm (usually over cities and open fields) and these can make a plane rise. And cool air can give you downdrafts (usually over wooded areas or water) and these make a plane drop until the propellers pull you out of it."

But Mr. Smith assured Bill there was no need to worry. He had designed enough planes to know how many safety devices they carried. "There's an indicator for air speed," he said, "and an *altimeter* to tell the pilot by air pressure how high he is above sea level, and a chemical sprayer near the hub of the propeller to prevent its blades from icing,

UPDRAFTS OF WARM AIR MAKE A PLANE RISE          DOWNDRAFTS, WHERE THE AIR IS COOL, MAKE THE PLANE DROP

and a device for showing the direction of ground radio stations, and rubber tubes along the edges of the wings through which air can be pumped to crack any ice that might form, and a gyro-compass to tell the pilot in what direction he is flying, and gauges to measure rate of flow and quantity of fuel, and a *gyro-horizon* to indicate when a plane is tipped, climbing or diving, and an *inclinator* to show the angle of ascent and descent, and a rate-of-climb indicator, and a *tachometer* to count the number of revolutions of the engine's crankshaft, a two-way radio, a pointer and ball floating in a liquid to tell the pilot whether he is making a correct turn, and an instrument to tell how many feet per minute a plane is climbing."

"Is that all?"

"No," Mr. Smith said. "There's the *automatic pilot*, which keeps the plane on course without anyone handling the controls. If the plane dips or swerves, it adjusts the rudder and wing flaps. Two gyroscopes that respond to movements of the plane are its chief parts."

"Like the kind of toy gyroscope some aunt or uncle always sends for Christmas?"

"Somewhat. So don't be frightened of these flying horses. You'll have a fine trip."

## Jets and Rockets

And Bill did. About an hour out of Central City they passed over a military air base. Below he saw another plane streak through the sky.

"There wasn't any propeller on that jet!" Bill cried.

Mr. Smith nodded. "A jet flies just the way a toy balloon swerves through the room when the balloon slips out of your hand and the air escapes.

"Air enters the front of the engine in a jet plane," Mr. Smith explained, "where a compressor operated by a gas turbine (revolving shaft) increases its pressure. This compressed air then goes into a combustion chamber where fuel is added. Air and fuel burn quickly and the gases given off are sent through a turbine. The heat of these gases may exceed 1500 degrees Fahrenheit although at high altitudes the air entering the engine may be 50 degrees below zero."

"What kind of fuel is used?" Bill asked.

"Usually low quality stuff like kerosene."

"What happens in the turbine?"

HOW A JET WORKS

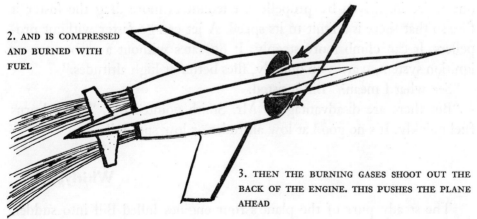

1. AIR IS SCOOPED INTO THE ENGINE HERE

2. AND IS COMPRESSED AND BURNED WITH FUEL

3. THEN THE BURNING GASES SHOOT OUT THE BACK OF THE ENGINE. THIS PUSHES THE PLANE AHEAD

"The hot gases cause the turbine to spin, about ten thousand revolutions per minute," Mr. Smith replied. "This provides the power to work the air compressor and to generate electricity for the lights and radio. The gases then pass through pipes to a nozzle at the rear of the plane. They flow even faster. The air rushing out of the nozzle makes the plane move forward."

"I don't get it," Bill said.

"Now think," Mr. Smith remarked patiently. "What happens when you balance on a bike and push back with your feet?"

"I move forward."

"So you get the forward movement from a thrust in the opposite direction."

"That's so!"

"And a jet plane moves forward from the thrust of gases moving in the opposite direction."

"It's that simple?"

"In theory, yes. A rocket works on this same principle of what we call a *reaction engine*, but a rocket carries all its own fuel whereas a jet must take in air as well as carry fuel."

"Yet jet planes burn cheap fuel," Bill said. "Why use any other kind of plane?"

"Cheap fuel is an advantage," Mr. Smith admitted. "A plane like the one we're in, driven by propellers, encounters more drag the faster it flies so that there is a limit to its speed. A jet can go faster without propellers. It can climb more steeply. It operates without a carburetor or ignition system, warms up quickly, flies better at high altitudes."

"See what I mean?" Bill insisted.

"But there are disadvantages," Mr. Smith pointed out. "A jet burns fuel quickly. It's no good at low altitudes or low speeds."

## Whirlybirds

The steady purr of the plane's four engines lulled Bill into sudden drowsiness. He looked down on white clouds flecked with golden glints from the sun, blinking his eyes in an effort to stay awake. Mr. Smith peered over the boy's shoulder and said:

"Look there—to your right. That's my favorite kind of plane."

"A whirlybird!" Bill said.

"Or a Flying Windmill, which was the first nickname a helicopter had." Mr. Smith smiled at a memory. "When I was wounded in World War II there was no sight more pleasant than one of those planes, hovering like a hummingbird over the battlefield. That's how I got back to the base hospital. Maybe that's why I'm alive today."

"A whirlybird can fly any way—up, down, forward, backward, right, left, or hang in one spot, can't it?" Bill asked.

"Yes, indeed. As early as 1500," Mr. Smith said, "Leonardo da Vinci designed a helicopter—without an engine, of course. But it wasn't until 1910 that a Russian-born, naturalized American citizen, Igor Sikorsky, built a helicopter capable of lifting its own weight. Unhappily, when the weight of a pilot was added, Sikorsky's machine wouldn't rise. A Frenchman, Louis Charles Breguet, overcame the problem of lifting pilot and plane, and soon others were demonstrating the extraordinary possibilities in this aircraft. By 1939 a German, Ewald Rohlfs, was flying a whirlybird at 11,700 feet."

"You don't have propellers on a jet or wings on a helicopter," Bill observed.

Mr. Smith nodded. "The wide, long blades of the propeller (called a *rotor*) on top of the helicopter lift the plane. The blades, turning parallel with the ground instead of at right angles to it, are curved on top. Thus the air travels faster over the top, lessening the air pressure," Mr. Smith explained. "That gives you lift. The plane flies in whatever direction you tilt those blades. Since a helicopter does not depend on a forward motion for lift—an ordinary plane falls if there is not sufficient air flowing under its wings—all a helicopter must do to hang in the air is to balance evenly the lift of its rotor and the downward pull of gravity.

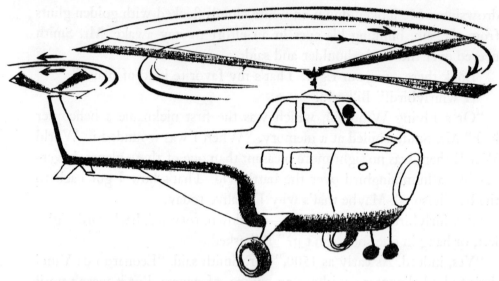

THE TWO ROTORS TURN IN OPPOSITE DIRECTIONS

"Igor Sikorsky solved the big problem in making helicopters," Mr. Smith continued. "If you had designed helicopters in the early 1920's you would have worried over what engineers call *torque pull*. You remember the old problem with an ordinary plane—that the propellers revolving in one direction tend to turn the fuselage in the opposite direction? This is another example of torque pull. And when the rotor blades turn to the left, the helicopter tends to turn to the right. Sikorsky's solution was to put a small propeller on the left side, near the tail, that, turning at a right angle to the earth, balanced out the torque pull. Two rotors turning in opposite directions do the same thing. We call that model an 'egg beater.' "

"There's an answer to everything," Bill declared.

"If you work at it long enough and hard enough," Mr. Smith said.

Bill grew conscious that the plane was losing altitude. Then the light flashed on in front: FASTEN SEAT BELTS.

"Well," said Mr. Smith with a laugh, "your flying horses are almost there. Not bad, eh?"

Bill just grinned.

# 7. The ALL-SEEING EYE: Untangling the Mysteries of the Universe

EVERY year when school started Bill worried that his new teacher would be a bust. And every year, within a week, Bill had to admit he was wrong. Miss Craig proved no exception.

Take the day she arrived with the old camera, magnifying glass, and long cardboard tube. These objects she placed on her desk with a mysterious smile and asked: "Who was Galileo?"

"Well, who was he?" Bill demanded.

"An Italian who lived in the early 1600's," Miss Craig answered. "His full name was Galileo Galilei. Sounds like a school cheer, doesn't it? His father, who wanted Galileo to be a doctor, had a hard time with the boy. He painted or played on the lute and organ. Or he sat in the cathedral at Pisa watching the great lamp swing from the ceiling while his mind worked out the theory of the pendulum and how he could time the swinging of the lamp by his pulse-beat."

"Galileo must have been quite a guy," Bill said.

"Yes," Miss Craig agreed, "but in his own way he was a trouble-maker. One day he climbed to the top of the Leaning Tower of Pisa and announced that he would prove all the professors at the university wrong in one belief. *They* said that if you dropped a ten-pound weight and a one-pound weight from the tower, the heavier object would fall ten times faster, but *he* said that all objects the same shape and size, no matter how much they weighed, fell at the same speed. And he proved that he was right. Galileo made other surprising discoveries. He declared that the moon didn't shine by its own light. He insisted that the Milky Way was a mass of stars—how many, no one could say. And he aroused great anger by supporting the belief that the earth moved around the sun.

"Galileo wouldn't change his mind to please his enemies," Miss Craig continued. "He had seen into mysteries that they knew nothing about. A Dutch scientist named Hans Lippershey had invented the telescope, so Galileo made a telescope—as we are going to do right now!"

GALILEO CLIMBED TO THE TOP OF THE LEANING TOWER

## Making Your Own Telescope

Miss Craig called Bill to her desk.

"First," she instructed, "cut the cardboard tube into two sections; then roll one section again so that it will be small enough to fit snugly inside the other tube."

Bill cut the tube, rewound one section, and slid it into the other. He took a small, thick convex lens and a large, thin convex lens from the camera and magnifying glass. Miss Craig had him fit the small lens into the rewound section of the tube to serve as his *eye-piece lens* and the large lens went into the other section to serve as his *objective lens*. Scotch tape held both in place.

"Now," Miss Craig said, "slide the smaller tube in and out until the object you wish to see becomes clear."

To Bill's delight, his homemade telescope worked. It seemed almost too simple, but the first telescope Galileo had made was also crude, and during his lifetime Galileo never made a telescope that magnified an object more than thirty-three times. Even so, he discovered mountains and craters on the moon, the rings around the planet Saturn, and four of the moons of the planet Jupiter.

"Modern astronomers," Miss Craig said, "use two kinds of telescopes. One is the *refracting telescope*. In its eyepiece (or *ocular*) end there are two lenses—one for seeing the image and one for magnifying it. The objective lens at the other end may be as large as forty inches in diameter. This lens gathers the light from a star or planet in the sky, and bends those light rays into one bright *focal point*. Actually the image is turned upside down by the objective lens and seen upside down by the eyepiece. It's really like standing on your feet and your head at the same time," Miss Craig said.

"The other type of telescope is a *reflecting telescope*. A mirror rather than a glass is used in its objective end. Much larger objects can be reflected in the mirror. But the kind of telescope Bill has made will do for the contest I have in mind," Miss Craig announced. She had brought

HOW TO MAKE YOUR OWN TELESCOPE

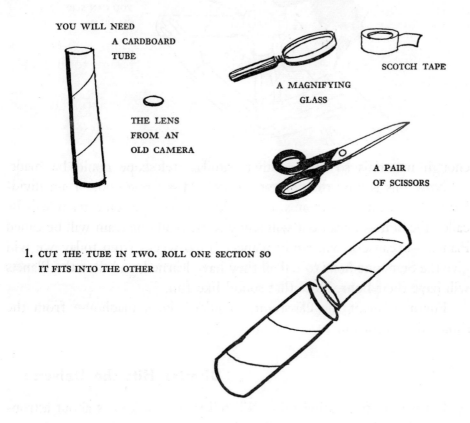

YOU WILL NEED
A CARDBOARD
TUBE

THE LENS
FROM AN
OLD CAMERA

A MAGNIFYING
GLASS

SCOTCH TAPE

A PAIR
OF SCISSORS

1. CUT THE TUBE IN TWO. ROLL ONE SECTION SO
   IT FITS INTO THE OTHER

2. FIT THE SMALL, THICK LENS INTO THE SMALL END, THE
   LARGER LENS (FROM THE MAGNIFYING GLASS) INTO THE
   LARGE END

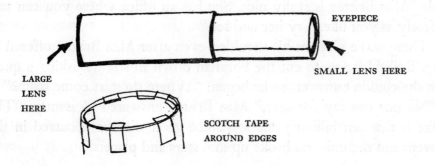

EYEPIECE

SMALL LENS HERE

LARGE
LENS
HERE

SCOTCH TAPE
AROUND EDGES

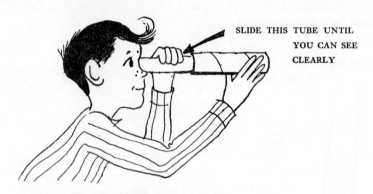

SLIDE THIS TUBE UNTIL
YOU CAN SEE
CLEARLY

enough materials so that another, similar, telescope could be made.

"Now this is how the contest works," Miss Craig said. "I am dividing the class into two teams, each with a telescope. One team will be called the Stars—because it will study stars. And one team will be called Planets—because it will study planets. Two weeks from today we will give the Stars one hour to tell all they have learned, and then the Planets will have their hour. Does that sound like fun?"

For a moment the classroom sounded like a madhouse from the shouts that went up.

### Disaster Hits the Universe

Bill was a Star. Father said: "I'll tell you who knows about astronomy—Miss Bristoe, our town librarian."

Bill frowned. He saw Miss Bristoe as a tyrant waiting to club him over the head if he talked too loud. Mother guessed his thought and said: "Miss Bristoe is really nice. She has an office where you can talk as freely as you like. Try her and see."

There was a chip on his shoulder, even after Miss Bristoe offered to help. Bill's idea was to cut the librarian down to size by asking a question she couldn't answer, so he began: "Where do stars come from?"

"No one can say for sure," Miss Bristoe answered pleasantly. "The belief is that ten billion years ago some great disaster occurred in the heavens and the universe broke up into stars and planets."

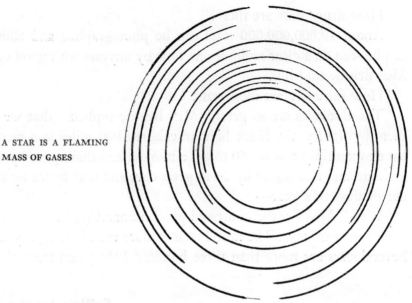

A STAR IS A FLAMING
MASS OF GASES

"But what is a star?"

"A sun."

"As large as the sun around which the earth turns?"

Miss Bristoe thought. "The best guess," she said, "is that if you could bore a hole through our sun, the hole would be 865,000 miles deep. Most stars would measure less than 25,000 miles, but a giant star called Betelgeuse would give you a hole of 200,000,000 miles and a star called Epsilon Aurigae would give you a hole of 2,400,000,000 miles!"

Bill had to respect anyone who could pop off an answer like that. "Is a star a burning mass of gases like the sun?"

Miss Bristoe nodded. "By using telescopes," she said, "astronomers collect light from the stars, and by using an instrument called a *spectograph* they can break up that light into various colors. These bands of color indicate the chemical elements in stars—for the most part, hydrogen, helium, calcium, and iron—and also the temperature of stars, which have a surface heat of from 5,000 to 25,000 degrees Fahrenheit although some may go as high as 100,000 degrees Fahrenheit and as low as 3,500 degrees Fahrenheit."

"How many stars are there?"

"About 30,000,000,000 stars can be photographed and about 3,000 can be seen on a clear night at one time by anyone with good eyesight," Miss Bristoe told Bill.

"How far away are most stars?"

"The distances are so great," Miss Bristoe replied, "that we measure them by *light years*. Since light travels 186,000 miles in a second, you have to multiply that by 60 to get a minute, and that figure by 60 to get an hour, and that figure by 24 to get a day, and that figure by the number of days in a year—

"Well," Miss Bristoe confessed good-humoredly, "I just couldn't do it without a mistake. The nearest star is more than four light years away. Several stars are more than three hundred light years from the earth."

### Sailing by the Stars

"By studying photographs of stars," Miss Bristoe said, "astronomers have come to believe that the rotation of the earth makes them rise and set. We know that stars move in two ways—by *proper motion*, which means that they move across our line of vision as the stars in the Big Dipper do, and by *radial motion*, which means that they move toward or away from us along our line of vision."

"How fast do they move?"

"Anywhere from twelve to two hundred miles a second. Stars are grouped into galaxies, of which our galaxy is but one of millions in the universe. Our sun moves around the center of its galaxy at a speed of 170 miles a second, and the earth moving with it makes a complete circle around the center of its galaxy once in about 225 million years."

If Bill were sailing a ship on a vast ocean, Miss Bristoe told him, the stars could lead him to land.

"How?"

"You bring your telescope tonight and I'll show you," the librarian offered.

Father and Mother came with Bill. They stood on the steps of the library, which Miss Bristoe called the deck of her ship. It was a fine, clear, bright night, and Bill never forgot his lesson that evening in navigating by the stars.

"In the Northern Hemisphere," Miss Bristoe said, "the two stars that are the pointers of the Big Dipper will tell you the position of Polaris, the polestar, which is never more than a degree away from true north. And the stars Altair and Procyon always rise and set less than ten degrees north of east and west. In the Southern Hemisphere there is no polestar, although the Southern Cross is thirty degrees from the south pole and can be used. Again Altair and Procyon give you east and west."

Miss Bristoe was filled with facts about stars. She told Bill and his parents that in ancient times people grouped the stars by the figures they appeared to make in the sky—bears, fishes, a bull, or a winged horse. About 150 A. D. an astronomer, Claudius Ptolemy, grouped stars by their brightness into *magnitudes*, of which there are five. Since the North Star is di-

THE BIG DIPPER AND THE POLE STAR

rectly over the earth, the earth's rotation does not affect its position. And since the light waves at the edge of a beam travel through different thicknesses of air, these waves come to us in irregular patterns and make us think that stars "twinkle."

## All About Planets

When the day came for Bill, as spokesman for the Stars, to tell the class all his team had learned, he said that their best friend had been Miss Bristoe. Cy Peters, who had been afflicted with polio and leaned on a crutch when he spoke, also said that his team, the Planets, owed special appreciation to the librarian. When Cy talked, he became so interesting that everyone watched his face and never thought about the crutch.

"Nine planets," Cy began, "revolve around the sun. The Earth is one of these planets, and the others are Mercury, Mars, Venus, Pluto, Uranus, Neptune, Saturn, and Jupiter.

"*Planet* is an old Greek word," Cy said. "It means *wanderer*. And planets do move—they frequently change position. Early in 1500 a Polish astronomer, Nicholas Copernicus, was the first to show that the sun was the center of the solar system with the earth revolving around it. Until then people believed that the earth was the center of the universe."

"How can you tell a planet from a star?" someone asked.

Cy said that through a telescope a planet looked like a disc and distant stars like points of light. Stars twinkle and planets seem to glow. Stars give off their own light and planets reflect light from the sun.

Mercury, the smallest planet, is one-sixteenth the size of the earth, and Jupiter is 1,300 times as large as the earth. Cy put on the blackboard a chart that told the class many things about planets:

| PLANET | DISTANCE FROM SUN | PERIOD OF ORBIT | DIAMETER IN MILES |
|---|---|---|---|
| Mercury | .4 | 3 months | 3,100 |
| Venus | .7 | 7½ months | 7,700 |
| Earth | 1.0 | 1 year | 7,918 |
| Mars | 1.5 | 1 year, 10 months | 4,200 |
| Jupiter | 5.2 | 11.9 years | 86,700 |
| Saturn | 9.5 | 29.5 years | 71,500 |
| Uranus | 19.2 | 84 years | 32,000 |
| Neptune | 30.1 | 164.8 years | 31,000 |
| Pluto | 39.5 | 248.5 years | 4,000 |

"The distance of planets," Cy explained, "is measured in *astronomical units*. Since the earth is 92,000,000 miles from the sun, astronomers make that distance equal to one unit. The period of orbit is the time it takes a planet to go around the sun. Planets are classed into two groups. The *terrestrial* planets—Mercury, Venus, Earth and Mars—are so called be-

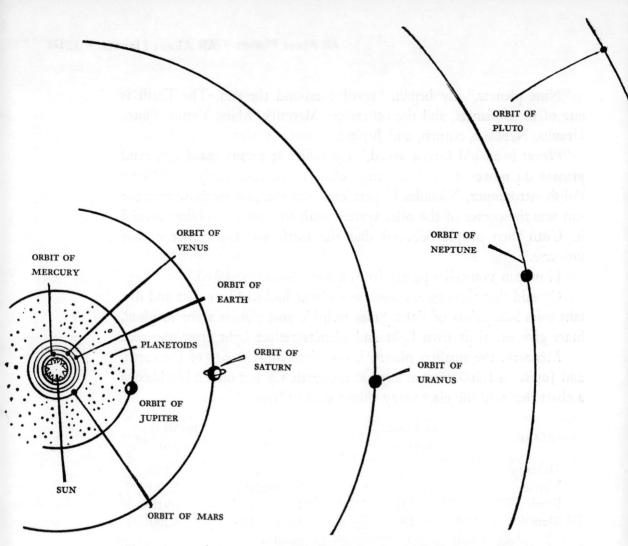

ORBIT OF
PLUTO

ORBIT OF
VENUS

ORBIT OF
MERCURY

ORBIT OF
NEPTUNE

ORBIT OF
EARTH

PLANETOIDS

ORBIT OF
SATURN

ORBIT OF
JUPITER

ORBIT OF
URANUS

SUN

ORBIT OF MARS

THE FOUR TERRESTRIAL PLANETS ARE WARMED BY THE SUN.
THE OUTER PLANETS ARE SO FAR AWAY THEY ARE ALWAYS HUNDREDS OF DEGREES BELOW ZERO.

cause they include the Earth. The others, because of their size, are called *major* planets. Between the planets are lots of small planets called *asteroids* or *planetoids* that are three astronomical units from the sun and orbit in from three to nine years."

## Planets Are Funny Places

Then Cy came to the part he liked best—what it would be like to live on another planet. "A boy weighing 100 pounds on earth would weigh 38 pounds on Mars and 260 pounds on Jupiter. Mars would be great for a baseball player—he could heave a ball three times farther than on earth—but on Jupiter he could throw it only two-fifths as far, and maybe that's where some of the Big League teams did their spring training this year."

Planet by planet, here are more facts Cy had gathered:

*Mercury*—the hottest planet, with the temperature on its sunny side between 770 and 500 degrees Fahrenheit. Its atmosphere, if any, must be very thin. If you weighed 150 pounds on earth, you would weigh 40 pounds on Mercury.

*Venus*—the brightest planet. It has an atmosphere. Its temperatures in the sun range from 120 to 140 degrees Fahrenheit, if a cloud level isn't keeping us from getting the temperature on the planet's surface. Clouds completely surround it.

*Mars*—probably there is plant life here. It is more like the earth than other planets. Its color, as we see it, is fiery red. Has polar caps that melt during the summer. Its atmosphere contains less oxygen and water than our own. There are no oceans and the humidity is about the same as on our great deserts. Man as we know him could not live here.

*Jupiter*—largest of the planets and next brightest. Its day is half as long as ours. Clouds that may have temperatures of 225 degrees Fahrenheit below zero hide its real surface. It has eleven moons.

*Saturn*—looks like a big yellow star. It is so light that if placed on our earth it would float. Its temperature is always about 250 degrees Fahrenheit below zero. Three large rings merging to look like a halo surround Saturn, and each ring is composed of particles of destroyed moons. Nine planets surround it. Its days are 10¼ hours long.

*Uranus*—may still be partially gaseous. We see it as a pale green orb. Its temperature is about 300 degrees Fahrenheit below zero. Four moons surround it, and move in the opposite direction from most solar bodies—that is, from east to west.

*Neptune*—very little known about it. Can never be seen with the naked eye. May rotate on its axis once every sixteen hours. Looks like a small green globe and its probable temperature is 300 degrees Fahrenheit below zero. Has one moon, also rotating (like the moons on Uranus) from east to west.

*Pluto*—not discovered until 1930. We see it as a yellowish mass. It is cold and dry.

## The Planet We Know Best

Both Bill and Cy, declared Miss Craig, had done well in presenting the story of the stars and the planets. She also had been working these past two weeks studying about the earth.

"As Bill told us," the teacher said, "some sort of disaster occurred in the universe billions of years ago, and the earth was formed—a mass that is almost completely round, for its diameter at the equator is about twenty-seven miles more than its diameter through the North and South poles. If you weighed the earth, you would need scales that could measure 6,000 million million million tons! Gravity—that force that pulls things to the ground—holds the atmosphere on the earth and even the moon in its path about the earth."

That word *atmosphere* was one Miss Craig wished them to remember, for it was one of the three major things that made up the earth. Simply described, it is an "air blanket" about two hundred miles thick. The lower atmosphere (*troposphere*)—between six and seven miles above sea level—contains the clouds and winds. The next layer of air—reaching to twenty-five miles above sea level—is the *stratosphere* and contains neither clouds, moisture, nor wind. Whereas the temperature of the lower atmosphere varies, that of the stratosphere remains an almost constantly sixty-seven degrees Fahrenheit below zero.

"Now number two among the major divisions of the earth," Miss Craig said, "is the water areas or *hydrosphere*. Three-quarters of the earth's surface—about 141,300,000 square miles—are covered by oceans, seas, lakes, rivers. The average depth of all the oceans is 2½ miles.

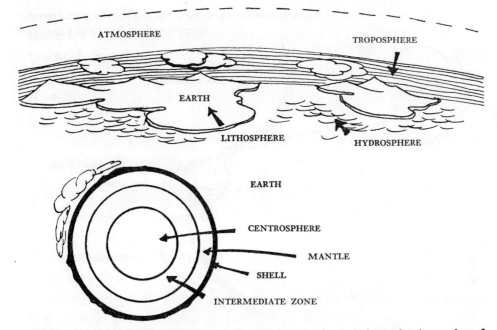

"The last major division, the *lithosphere*, is the solid earth. A study of earthquake waves has taught us that there are four zones between the surface (or *outer shell*) of the earth and its center (or *centrosphere*). Immediately beneath the outer shell is the *mantle* and beneath the mantle is the *intermediate zone*. The thickness of the outer shell averages thirty-seven miles with Mt. Everest, its highest point, rising 29,141 feet above sea level, and the Philippine Deep, its lowest point, estimated at 35,400 feet below sea level. The mantle is thought to be about 750 miles thick, the intermediate zone 1,000 miles thick, and the center about 4,200 miles in diameter."

## We Are All Space Travelers

"Every being that lives on earth is a space traveler," Miss Craig said. "In fact, a man on earth moves in three directions at once!"

Everyone looked suspicious.

"Don't you believe me?" Miss Craig asked.

"Can you prove it?" Bill demanded.

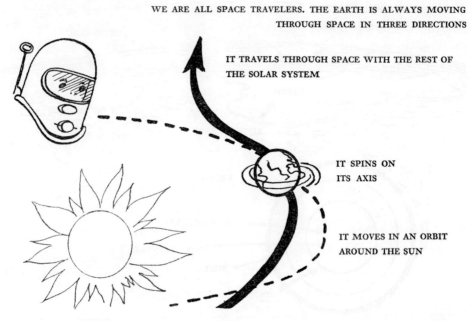

WE ARE ALL SPACE TRAVELERS. THE EARTH IS ALWAYS MOVING THROUGH SPACE IN THREE DIRECTIONS

IT TRAVELS THROUGH SPACE WITH THE REST OF THE SOLAR SYSTEM

IT SPINS ON ITS AXIS

IT MOVES IN AN ORBIT AROUND THE SUN

"Certainly. Once every 23 hours, 56 minutes, and 4.1 seconds the earth spins on its axis, dividing day from night. Don't you travel with it?"

"I must."

"And once every 365 days, 6 hours, 9 minutes, and 9.54 seconds the earth carries you around the sun, and to cover those 92,900,000 miles you travel 67,000 miles an hours—or 19 miles every second."

Bill stared.

"And," finished Miss Craig, "the earth and everybody on it travel with the entire solar system in the direction of the star Vega—and on that trip you cover 43,000 miles an hour!"

"No wonder Father tells me sometimes I don't know where I'm going," Bill chuckled.

"Well, you do now," Miss Craig told him. "Animals with hair and warm blood," she said, "first became common on earth about 60,000,000 years ago. When the caveman appeared was a guess—some said about 2,000,000 years ago. Man needed his cave to hide from the huge animals, such as woolly rhinos, that roamed the earth. This period in the world's history is called the Ice Age, for glaciers often covered large parts of North America and Europe. Between 15,000 and 25,000 years ago the glaciers melted and climates grew warmer. In the East the land rose, pushing back the ocean. Man began to wander into all areas of our planet."

## A Few Drops of Water

Next morning Bill set off for school, filled with a sense of adventure. Miss Craig was a fine teacher. And there on Miss Craig's desk was another discovery that gave man his all-seeing eyes—a microscope!

"I want you each to look into the microscope at the slide already there," Miss Craig invited.

Bill squinted into the microscope. He saw wiggling animals with six legs, and plants that looked like the wavy lines he made when he tested a fountain pen to see if it would write, and round, live blobs with long, thin tails that moved them along.

"What is it?" he asked.

"A few drops of water from the pond behind the school," Miss Craig answered.

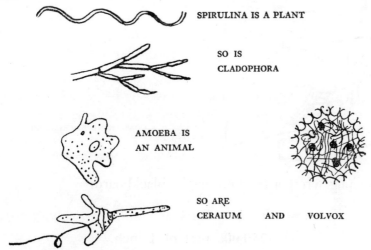

SPIRULINA IS A PLANT

SO IS CLADOPHORA

AMOEBA IS AN ANIMAL

SO ARE CERAIUM AND VOLVOX

IF YOU LOOK THROUGH A MICROSCOPE YOU MIGHT SEE ALL THESE THINGS IN A DROP OF POND WATER

"You mean all this is in *that* water?"

The teacher nodded. "A Dutch spectacle-maker, Zacarias Janssen, made the first compound microscope in 1590," she said, "and since then many scientists have worked to produce this wonderful instrument you are now using.

"Like the telescope," Miss Craig continued, "a microscope bends light rays. In its simplest form, a microscope is no more than a magnifying glass attached to a holder. The compound microscope, like this one, has two lenses—the *eyepiece* and the *objective* lens mounted at opposite ends of an adjustable tube."

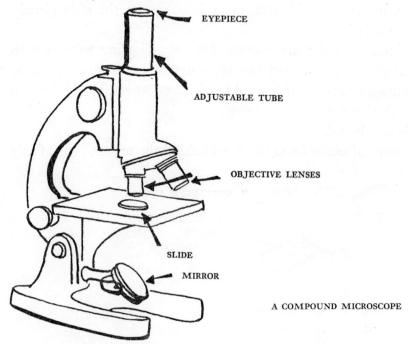

EYEPIECE

ADJUSTABLE TUBE

OBJECTIVE LENSES

SLIDE

MIRROR

A COMPOUND MICROSCOPE

Miss Craig wrote a fraction on the blackboard:

$$\frac{1}{250,000} \text{ part of 1 inch.}$$

"That," she said, "is the size of a germ that can be seen through the most powerful microscope. Once we could explore into the unseen and unknown," Miss Craig pointed out, "we could discover the tiny germs that caused diseases like typhoid fever, malaria, diphtheria, and small-pox. We could learn about the structure of plants—and even watch them growing! And we discovered tiny plants that caused diseases."

"Why," Bill exclaimed, "that sounds like the greatest detective job there is!"

Bill was right, Miss Craig said, although science gave another name—*bacteriology*—to the methods used for detecting disease-causing organisms (or *bacteria*) invisible to the naked eye.

## Better Than Sherlock Holmes

"Sometimes when you use a microscope to magnify bacteria a thousand times they still look no bigger than a pencil point," Miss Craig declared. "And, under a microscope," she said, "you discover there are all kinds of bacteria."

Within a few days, Bill thought, the school doctor would examine them. And the school nurse would make sure they had their shots against polio and smallpox. And the school dentist would see that their teeth were healthy. It was like an army, in his school, in all schools, at war against disease. But none of this big, exciting drama could have been possible unless Janssen had made the compound microscope!

"And a German named Robert Koch was a much better detective than Sherlock Holmes," Miss Craig added. "You remember how Sherlock Holmes always went after his criminals by observing small details—cigarette ash, fingerprints, a bit of hair? Well, Koch worked out methods for going after the invisible killers, or bacteria, far more thoroughly."

Every infectious disease, Koch believed, was caused by a specific germ (bacteria). To prove his theory he devoted long years to searching for the germ responsible for tuberculosis of the lungs. He took blood samples from persons stricken with this disease, and in time discovered the germ that he was sure had caused the illness. He isolated this germ or bacteria where no other living substance could touch it, and thus was able to raise a kind of family of this germ. Now if he took a healthy animal and injected the germ into its body, would it develop the disease? Koch's experiments demonstrated that it would, and the germ theory of infectious disease, once proved, revolutionized all medicine!

"Others working in bacteriology," Miss Craig said, "proved, like Koch, to be better detectives than Sherlock Holmes. One you should certainly remember every time you drink a glass of milk is the Frenchman, Louis Pasteur."

"I bet," Bill cried, "he's the guy behind *pasteurized* milk!"

"Indeed he was," Miss Craig answered. "No one can say how many million human lives Louis Pasteur saved. Once people believed in 'spontaneous generation'—that is, that disease-causing organisms spring out of nowhere. But Pasteur said no—germs came from the air, or from chem-

PASTEUR BELIEVED THAT GERMS COULD BE KILLED

ical changes in liquids. Moreover he believed that germs could be killed and their spread prevented."

## Saving a Boy's Life

"Louis Pasteur was already famous by 1880. He had studied the diseases of animals—anthrax in cattle and sheep, and chicken cholera—and had proved that through vaccination he could prevent and cure such illnesses. One dreadful disease called hydrophobia or rabies, spread by the bite of a mad dog, he had cured in animals. Could he cure it in human beings?

"On a hot day in July 1885 a woman knocked frantically on Pasteur's door. With her was a nine-year-old boy.

" 'Monsieur,' she cried, 'my little Joseph has been bitten by a mad dog. Two days ago, when Joseph was going to school, the wicked creature leaped on the child. Look how he was bitten, Monsieur—in fourteen places!'

"Poor Joseph Meister was a sick and frightened boy—that Pasteur could not deny. He had the lad put to bed while he consulted with other scientists. Dare he try his serum that cured rabies in animals upon a human being?

" 'Try the serum,' they said. 'It is his only chance.' "

Bill raised his hand, interrupting Miss Craig's story. "What is a serum?"

The teacher thought that was a good question. "Some poisonous germs that cause disease are called *viruses*. These viruses are grown in a special fluid, then strained to gather the poisons, or *toxins*, and injected into an animal over several days, with each dose containing more poison or toxin. Dose by dose the animal builds up in its blood *antibodies*, or *antitoxins*, to resist the original poison. The serum is then made from the animal's blood.

"And it was a serum of this kind," Miss Craig said, "that Louis Pasteur used on Joseph Meister. It was the final doses he feared most.

All Paris followed the reports of the child's treatment, hoping and praying that the boy would live. The last dose, the strongest, Pasteur gave on the tenth day. He waited. He prayed. He almost cried with anxiety.

"But the miracle occurred. Joseph lived—the first human being cured of rabies by a serum—and in later years, with different serums, other human beings have been protected against cholera, diphtheria, lockjaw, and many more diseases! And of course Louis Pasteur kept right on with his work, demonstrating that, by heating and chilling liquids, bacteria could be kept from spoiling milk, cheese, wines."

"Then that's what we mean by pasteurization!" Bill guessed.

"True," Miss Craig said. "But behind these wonderful discoveries was the microscope. Man had to know first that his invisible enemies existed. Then he could conquer them."

Miss Craig looked down at her class. "Most of what we know about science we have learned in the last hundred years," she stated. "Imagine what boys and girls like you will know about the earth, our bodies, the stars and planets in another hundred years—perhaps in twenty-five or fifty."

Bill closed his eyes, caught in a dream. Zip—that was a plane half way across the sky. Pow—that was a space ship off to visit the moon. And he saw himself peering into a microscope and saying: "I've caught you"—meaning that another disease-bearing germ had been eliminated. A wonderful dream—and none of it impossible.

# 8. FUTURE UNLIMITED : Rockets, Satellites, and the Atomic Age

MANY afternoons Bill said: "I'm going to the library—see you for supper." Mother simply smiled and told Miss Bristoe in private: "You've surely made a friend of that boy."

"We're learning about the whole world of science," Miss Bristoe explained.

Bill told Mother about how all over the world scientists were working together to find the answers to great unsolved mysteries.

"Like what?" Mother asked.

"Well, like how fast glaciers are melting," Bill said. "After all, 10 per

133

cent of the earth's surface is still covered by glaciers and if this ice should melt, most of our coastal cities would be under several feet of water. Moreover, these glaciers, spilling 'cold fronts' on us, cause many patterns of weather. You can see that *glaciologists*," declared Bill, who liked a fancy word occasionally, "can teach us a great deal."

## Some Other Mysteries

And scientists who study *oceanography* are also engaged in other important work. About 70 per cent of the earth's surface is covered by water. When you think about fish as a source of food—and in some parts of the world fish are the main source—then it is worth knowing how long it takes a deep current in the ocean to move from the North Pole to South Pole. Is the answer 100 years or 10,000? How do these

SCIENTISTS USE AQUALUNGS, SUBMARINE CAMERA SLEDS, AND RADIOACTIVE TRACERS

currents affect our weather? And can quantities of harmful, radioactive materials in the atmosphere be dumped safely into the oceans?

"Scientists use aqualungs, submarine camera sleds, and radioactive tracers searching for answers to these questions," Bill explained. A scientist is more than a bald-headed fellow in a white smock who spends all day poking his nose into a test tube. A scientist could be a hardy explorer, willing to go anywhere. So you find scientists in airplanes, towing a round device called a *gravimeter* that records changes in gravity resulting from rock formations beneath the earth's surface. Or they climb mountains or go deep into caves seeking insight into the causes of earthquakes. Who can predict how many lives those fellows may one day save or how much property damage they might prevent?

"And take the crowd who make a special study of hurricane's tornadoes, and other forms of weather —the *meteorologists*," Bill said. "Why, you find those fellows on snow-capped mountaintops, or on the misty, storm-ridden Kerguelen Islands between South Africa and

OR THEY CLIMB MOUNTAINS . . .

Antartica where the only other living creatures are rats and mice. And how about those air currents above the earth that travel at speeds up to 150 miles an hour—those currents we call *jet streams?* Suppose we can chart their movement?" Bill demanded. "Think of the improvements that will bring into travel by air!"

And in case Mother needed further proof that Bill wasn't wasting his afternoons with Miss Bristoe, he went on to ask her: "Do we really know how the sun affects our lives? What causes sunburn or makes the colors fade in draperies?" Bill rushed on. "It's invisible rays, *cosmic rays*, from the sun! Look at the sun through a telescope when there's an atomic storm up there producing these cosmic rays, and you'll see flares of fire shooting off into space for as far as 100,000 miles! What effect do these sun storms have on our planet? Do they change our atmosphere? Do they, eh?"

Mother said: "Bill, every family needs a cook, maid, bottle washer and cleaner-upper. That's me. And in the world today, every family can use a bright, alert scientist. That's you. I think I'll stick to my job and let you become better at yours."

"A good deal," Bill said, grinning.

### All About Rockets

Sooner or later Bill was certain to find one headline on the front page of any newspaper—either the Americans or the Russians had a new satellite orbiting in outer space. To launch a satellite you began with a rocket, and so, sensibly, Miss Bristoe said:

"That's where we'll begin—with rockets.

"A rocket is simply a *reaction engine*. When you fire a gun and it kicks back against your shoulder, you get a reaction." Bill already knew that the same principle caused a jet plane to fly. "The first rocket-makers were the ancient Chinese," Miss Bristoe said, "and a tricky time they had with their fancy fireworks until they learned first that if the powder in a rocket doesn't burn evenly, it will turn in the wrong direction;

A ROCKET GOES BECAUSE THE BURNING GAS INSIDE HAS NOWHERE TO GO BUT
OUT THE BACK AND THIS PUSHES THE ROCKET FORWARD

and, second, that with cone-shaped or pointed heads rockets fly better than with blunt heads; and, finally, that a rocket needs its greatest burning power, or thrust, at the moment of launching.

"Over seven hundred years ago the Mongols besieged the Chinese in a town called Kai-fung-fu. 'Ah-ha,' said the Chinese, 'we'll teach you something new'—and they filled the air with flaming rockets. The horses of the Mongols reared up in fright. There was a virtual stampede till the riders realized that rockets as weapons were no more than nuisances. So the Mongols came back and licked the Chinese.

THE HORSES OF THE MONGOLS
REARED UP IN FRIGHT

"For the next seven hundred years," Miss Bristoe said, "rockets were tried with very little success as instruments of war. We know that the British used them in the War of 1812 for in our National Anthem we sing about 'the rockets' red glare.' By then we could build rockets that could travel more than a mile, principally by putting the stick that guided the rocket in the center of its base so that we could have five nozzles instead of one with which to power a rocket.

"Later it was found that you didn't need a stick to keep a rocket steady in flight. If a bullet

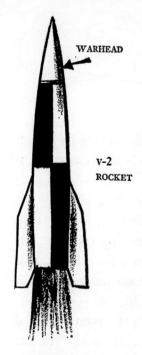

WARHEAD

V-2
ROCKET

traveled steadily because it turned in the air, then why couldn't the burning gases in a rocket strike a vane that would make it turn? The idea worked well —for short ranges, anyway. The trouble with rockets until recent times has been that they lacked accuracy."

Bill broke in: "But didn't the Germans bomb London with rockets during World War II?"

Miss Bristoe nodded. "Sadly enough, man in time learned how to transform rockets into deadly weapons. It was the second of the rocket bombs the Germans built—the *V-2*—that became the real terror.

"They stood a V-2 straight up on a platform and launched it like a skyrocket," the librarian said. "A chemical solution produced the steam to turn its engine. Pumps then forced liquid oxygen and alcohol from the gas tanks into the combustion chamber. The mixture burned so violently that the gases shooting out of the tail of a V-2 gave it a thrust equal to the force of twenty-two tons."

"How fast could it fly?"

"About three thousand miles an hour."

"How far?"

"About two hundred miles."

Miss Bristoe said that she didn't like to think of rockets killing people. At Cape Canaveral, Florida, when the Americans used a rocket to put a satellite into orbit—well, that was a great achievement, for science was looking for information that would enrich mankind's future.

## Launching a Satellite

"... 8 ... 7 ... 6 ..." Bill should think of himself, Miss Bristoe said, as inside the blockhouse at Cape Canaveral in the final seconds before a satellite is launched. On the firing table outside stands the three-stage rocket—seventy feet from tip to base. Inside the first stage the flame that will ignite the motor is already firing ...

"... 5 ... 4 ... 3 ..." The fuel pumps start up. Liquid oxygen and a very special mixture of distilled petroleum are held back by valves that will soon open. The cables drop off the rocket, and ...

"... 2 ... 1 .. 0 ..." The valves release, the fuel flows through pipes, the pumps force it into the motor ...

"... *Fire!* ..." For a moment, rising, the rocket seems to balance on its own exhaust blast.

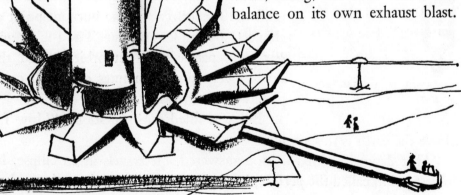

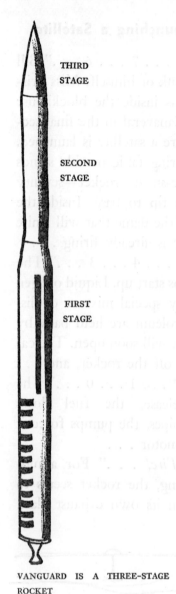

THIRD
STAGE

SECOND
STAGE

FIRST
STAGE

VANGUARD IS A THREE-STAGE
ROCKET

But it is moving up, up, *up*, so quickly that in ten, twelve, fifteen seconds it looks like a toy against the vast sky.

All eyes watch the radar screen. At about forty miles in the air—exactly one minute and a half after firing—the second stage should ignite and the first drop off. Another combination of fuels, of which nitric acid is a chief ingredient, should give the rocket a new, powerful thrust.

Now there are two dots on the radar screen. A voice cries out: "The first stage has separated!" The rocket soars faster. Ten minutes after takeoff the rocket can be two hundred miles above sea level and seven hundred miles from Cape Canaveral. At its peak the second stage will travel at about 8,600 miles an hour.

Now comes the movement when the third stage, carrying the satellite, ignites. A special solid fuel, burning at great intensity, gives an enormous thrust. Within instants the speed is 10,000, 11,000, 12,000 miles an hour until the rocket reaches the burnout point at about 17,000 miles an hour. The rocket and satellite separate, each in orbit around the earth. Every ninety minutes each will completely circle the earth.

Bill was filled with questions. "How far above the earth is this satellite?" he began.

"That depends," Miss Bristoe answered. "It travels in an ellipse. Its lowest point, called the *perigee*, is wherever it separates from the rocket.

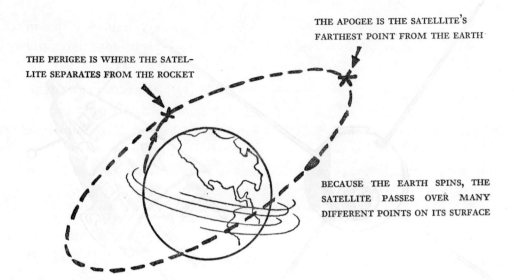

THE PERIGEE IS WHERE THE SATEL-
LITE SEPARATES FROM THE ROCKET

THE APOGEE IS THE SATELLITE'S
FARTHEST POINT FROM THE EARTH

BECAUSE THE EARTH SPINS, THE
SATELLITE PASSES OVER MANY
DIFFERENT POINTS ON ITS SURFACE

At its highest point, the *apogee*, it may be 1,600 miles or more above the earth."

"What makes the orbit move—I mean, why can't you see a satellite passing overhead every ninety minutes?"

"Because the earth revolves inside the orbit."

"How big was the first American satellite?"

"About twenty-one inches in diameter."

"What's in it?"

"Instruments to measure the temperature and the ultraviolet rays produced by storms on the sun. And microphones that pick up tiny solid particles that strike the satellite. And a pressure gauge to tell if these particles puncture the outer skin of the satellite. And a radio that transmits these measurements to earth as electrical signals. The four spike-like poles on the satellite are the antennae that help send radio signals."

Bill whistled. "What determines the low and high point of an orbit?"

"Man does. At present we keep the low point at a distance above the earth where the satellite forces its way through a few thousand miles of upper atmosphere. Thus it encounters a friction—called *orbital decay*—that in time diminishes its orbit and helps it to burn up."

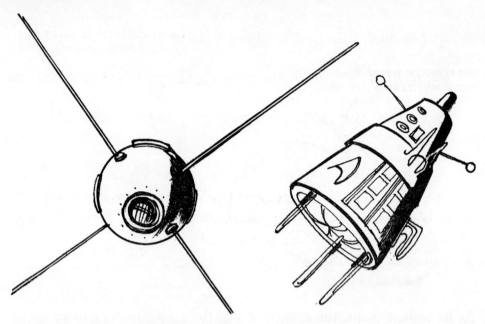

THERE ARE MANY INSTRUMENTS IN A SATELLITE, AND SATELLITES MAY BE DIFFERENT SHAPES

"Do we want it to?"

"Yes. When the time comes for us to launch space ships we won't want outer space filled with man-made satellites!"

"Couldn't we just shoot 'em down?"

"No. If a satellite is broken into a dozen pieces, each piece will orbit around the earth, unless the friction of the heavier atmosphere causes it to burn up."

"Like the particles of old moons that make the rings around Saturn?"

"Exactly."

"Does the orbit have to be an ellipse?"

"No. With a fourth stage to the rocket, we could make low point and high point equal and the satellite's orbit would become permanent."

Bill frowned. "It's tricky, expensive business. There should be other ways of launching a rocket."

"There are," Miss Bristoe told him. "One already being used is the *balloon-launch*, in which a thin, plastic balloon (often mistaken for a flying saucer) carries the rocket 100,000 or more feet about the earth before launching it. In time jet planes will very likely be used to launch rockets."

Bill said: "This talk about space ships—going to the moon and all that—do you believe it?"

"Of course," Miss Bristoe answered. "The future is unlimited."

## The Space Station

"What we learn from satellites," Miss Bristoe continued, "will help us to know what equipment is necessary for man to survive in outer space. Then the way will be open to launch a wheel-like space station in orbit around the earth."

"How would you get it there?" Bill demanded.

"In sections, probably. By remote control, we should be able to bring together those sections so that they can be assembled in outer space."

"How big would the station be?"

"Perhaps two hundred feet in diameter—large enough to house a crew of thirty or forty."

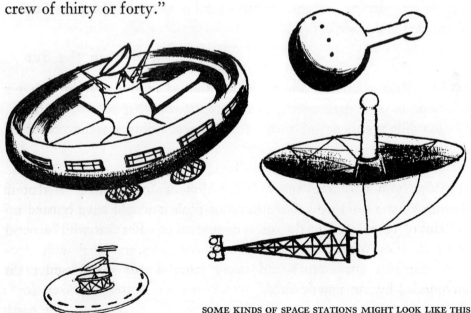

SOME KINDS OF SPACE STATIONS MIGHT LOOK LIKE THIS

"What would go into such a station?"

"Sleeping quarters, kitchen, dining room, telescopes, cameras, radio and television equipment, laboratories, water tanks—it would be quite a place!"

Bill believed it. Yet suppose fifty years ago somebody had told the Wright brothers that man would fly faster than sound travels, would they have believed it? Of course not! Yes, some day there would be space stations. Then astronomers could look through telescopes and solve many mysteries about the stars and planets! And meteorologists would uncover new secrets about the weather. Magnetism, gravity, cosmic rays—great forces governing life on our earth—would be understood more thoroughly. And the space station would be the jumping-off point for space ships to the moon and other planets!

Miss Bristoe said, "Think of our little man-made satellites, sending radio signals to stations around the world! How can the scientists of just one country study the atmosphere effectively when atmosphere is everywhere? So scientists all over the world work as teams—to study magnetism, glaciers, oceans, gravity, earthquakes, weather, the atmosphere, sun and cosmic rays!"

## Storms on the Sun

Miss Bristoe said: "When Galileo looked at the sun through his telescope he saw dark specks—called *sunspots*—that seemed to move. Galileo didn't understand them, for those sunspots are the center of dreadful storms on the sun."

"What kind of storms?"

"What you must remember, Bill," Miss Bristoe replied, "is that if the sun were a solid mass like a lump of coal, it would have burned up millions of years ago. But the sun is composed of gases that whirl around like terrific cyclones," she said. "And those gases are filled with electrical particles (or atoms) and every sunspot (or storm center) is surrounded by a magnetic field."

A HYDROGEN ATOM HAS ONLY ONE ELECTRON

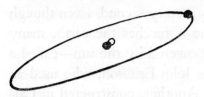

A HELIUM ATOM HAS TWO ELECTRONS

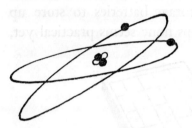

Bill sighed. He was back with his old friends, the ones that had started his interest in science—the + and — charges of electricity in the proton and electron of every atom!

"The simplest atom," Miss Bristoe told Bill, "is the hydrogen atom. It has 1 + charge and 1 — charge of electricity. It is like the cornerstone of a house. All other elements can be built upon it. Next in the range of simple atoms is the helium atom. And since the sun contains both hydrogen and helium, we can guess that one thing the sun's enormous heat is constantly doing is changing hydrogen into helium."

"And what happens?"

"Well, since the helium atom is lighter, something has to happen to what is lost in the process," Miss Bristoe answered, "and so it becomes light and heat radiated into space.

"Other transformations go on in the elements that compose the fiery sun. For example, when a carbon atom encounters the nucleus of a hydrogen atom, it produces a form of nitrogen that is radioactive. Then another proton (+ charge) strikes it and it changes into ordinary nitrogen. But now still another hydrogen proton strikes the ordinary nitrogen and changes that into a radioactive form of oxygen. And so the changes go on until the sun produces the hydrogen and helium with which it started!"

"It sounds like an atomic madhouse," Bill declared.

"It's very complicated," the librarian admitted.

"And yet," Bill said, "think of the enormous energy manufactured by the sun—if we only knew how to capture it!"

"A good scientific guess," Miss Bristoe said, "is that the sun's surface gives off about 70,000 horsepower of energy every second. Even though this energy is greatly diluted by the time it reaches the earth, many men have dreamed of building an engine powered by the sun—called a solar engine. One of the first to do so was John Ericsson, who used an 18-foot reflector to heat a six-inch boiler. Another, constructed in California in 1901, employed 1,788 small mirrors to heat a boiler. New models use aluminum mirrors and even storage batteries to store up power when the engine is not in use. Perhaps none seems practical yet,

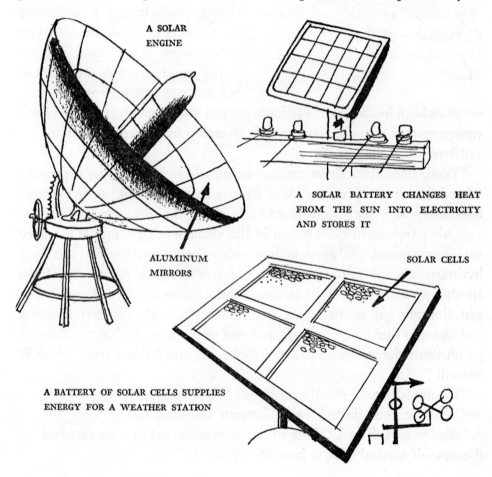

A SOLAR ENGINE

A SOLAR BATTERY CHANGES HEAT FROM THE SUN INTO ELECTRICITY AND STORES IT

ALUMINUM MIRRORS

SOLAR CELLS

A BATTERY OF SOLAR CELLS SUPPLIES ENERGY FOR A WEATHER STATION compared to a good diesel engine, and yet who can say what future method will be found to harness the energy of the sun?"

"And meanwhile, on a small scale, we have learned to produce atomic energy like the sun," Bill said.

## What Atomic Energy Is

"Since the days when the Greeks gave us the word atom—meaning *not cuttable*—man advanced slowly in his knowledge of the power hidden in the atom," Miss Bristoe said. "Only recently has he learned to make bombs of terrifying power. Whereas by burning a pound of carbon man can make 4.2 kilowatt hours of power, by splitting the atoms in a pound of an element called Uranium-235 (U-235) he can increase that amount of kilowatt hours of power 2,282,900 times!"

"Some difference!" Bill exclaimed. Then, with a grin, he asked: "Suppose I had to explain to my mother what energy is. What would I tell her?"

"In science," Miss Bristoe said, "you begin with the reason for things. How did we first discover there was a hidden source of energy? In 1896 a scientist in Paris named Henri Becquerel left a packet of unexposed photographic film near a piece of uranium ore. To his astonishment the film, when opened, was as darkened as though it had been exposed to light. Becquerel could only guess that some form of energy he didn't understand had darkened the film. This energy he named *radioactivity*."

"So," Bill said, "we begin with a mystery!"

"And a mystery we still had when Pierre and Marie Curie discovered radium," Miss Bristoe continued. "They knew that radium was highly radioactive. 'Why?' they asked—and couldn't say. Not until 1905 did the scientist Albert Einstein believe he had an answer—or a theory, which is a hunch to an answer. Said Einstein: 'Radioactivity is matter gradually changing into energy.'"

But scientists remained stubborn. The word atom meant "not cuttable" and atoms, they believed, could not be destroyed. A few were willing to be more open-minded on the subject. In the 1930's startling news came from Germany. Here three scientists indicated by chemical tests that the uranium atom could be split. Many discoveries about the atom were made, of a highly technical nature, and yet they added up to one extremely important fact—either by *fission* or *fusion* atomic energy could be released. "Now let me explain what I mean before you start beating out my brains with questions," Miss Bristoe said, laughing.

When atomic energy was produced by *fission*, Miss Bristoe explained, what happened had been expressed by Einstein in this formula:

$$E = MC^2$$

"What this means," the librarian continued, "is that when you split an atom the energy (E) equals (=) the matter destroyed (M) times the speed of light multiplied by itself ($C^2$). An atom when split gives off many small particles—or *neutrons*—which, striking other atoms, cause them to fly apart. In an atomic bomb, this *chain* reaction takes place in a fraction of a second, accounting for the tremendous destructive force of the bomb. For peace-time uses, the chain reaction takes place much more slowly in a specially constructed building called an *atomic reactor*."

"Is uranium the only element whose atoms can be changed into energy by fission?" Bill asked.

ATOMIC ENERGY IS MADE THROUGH FISSION WHEN FAST-MOVING ATOMIC PARTICLES SPLIT OTHER ATOMS APART

ATOMIC ENERGY IS MADE THROUGH FUSION WHEN THE NUCLEUS OF ONE ATOM JOINS WITH THE NUCLEUS OF ANOTHER

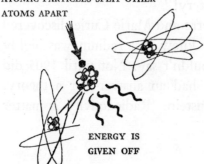

ENERGY IS GIVEN OFF

ENERGY IS GIVEN OFF

AN ATOMIC REACTOR MUST HAVE

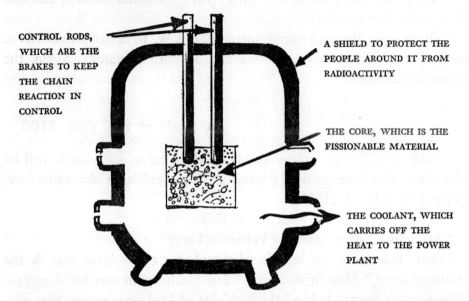

CONTROL RODS, WHICH ARE THE BRAKES TO KEEP THE CHAIN REACTION IN CONTROL

A SHIELD TO PROTECT THE PEOPLE AROUND IT FROM RADIOACTIVITY

THE CORE, WHICH IS THE FISSIONABLE MATERIAL

THE COOLANT, WHICH CARRIES OFF THE HEAT TO THE POWER PLANT

"The only one found in nature," Miss Bristoe said. "But by exposing metals called thorium and plutonium to a chain reaction, we can change them into forms of uranium."

"It's like the atomic hocus-pocus on the sun," Bill said.

"Man-made hocus-pocus," Miss Bristoe conceded.

"How does fusion work?"

"When atomic (or nuclear) energy is produced by *fusion*, the nucleus from one atom is fused with the nucleus of another atom. Hydrogen atoms of a special kind called hydrogen 2 and hydrogen 3 unite most easily. Again, what is happening on the sun occurs here. There is a difference in weight between the atoms, and when they unite, the weight left over becomes energy."

"Does Einstein's formula of $E = MC^2$ still apply?" Bill asked.

"Yes. And of course to create nuclear energy by fusion requires temperatures almost like those on the sun."

"Where on earth can you find temperatures like that?"

"In an atom bomb."

"You mean, atom bomb and then hydrogen bomb—it was like one duck following another?"

"That's right. But you must remember, Bill, we have just scratched the surface of understanding what we can do with the atom. Again, the future is unlimited."

## A Peek at the Year 2100

Suddenly Bill was entranced. "I wonder," he said, "what it will be like with atomic energy used generally. What will it be like, right *here*, in the year 2000 or 2100?"

"In fancy, let's take a peek," Miss Bristoe said.

"All right," Bill answered. "What do I see?"

"First, the enormous building beyond the city's limit that is the atomic reactor," Miss Bristoe said. "The machines in that building produce nuclear energy behind thick shields of lead or concrete that prevent harmful radioactive materials from escaping. From this plant comes the power to light and heat our homes and turn the machines in our factories. Smaller atomic 'plants' will power steamships and airplanes for distances and at speeds otherwise impossible.

"But tremendous power may be the least of the advantages we gain from atomic energy," Miss Bristoe declared. "Radioactivity is foe or friend, depending on how it is controlled. Through radioactivity we secure *isotopes*, which are substances (like gold, cobalt, and iodine) that have been

WHAT MAKES AN ISOTOPE?

AN ATOM'S WEIGHT IS DECIDED BY THE NUMBER OF PROTONS IN ITS NUCLEUS

A NORMAL HYDROGEN ATOM HAS ONE ELECTRON, ONE PROTON

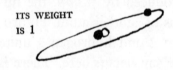

ITS WEIGHT
IS 1

BUT IF, BY ATOMIC BOMBARDMENT, ANOTHER PROTON IS ADDED TO THE NUCLEUS, ITS WEIGHT WOULD BE 2

THIS HYDROGEN ATOM IS AN ISOTOPE

made radioactive in an atomic reactor. Such isotopes give off rays—some that vanish almost instantly; others may last five thousand years."

"And isotopes are important?" Bill asked.

The librarian reached for a pad, and while Bill watched, wrote out this list:

## HOW WE CAN USE ISOTOPES

*In medicine*—to treat cancer, diseases of the blood cells, to regulate treatment by X-ray machines (which can be harmful), and in other ways to prolong man's life on earth.

*In agriculture*—to solve the mystery of how plants live and grow (by even duplicating perhaps the sun's effect on plants), to change and improve inherited characteristics in plants and animals so that they can resist blights and diseases, to control insects and strengthen fertilizers.

*In industry*—to secure closer measurements of metals, to produce new chemicals that will give us better rubber and plastics (as two examples), to prevent accidents (since an isotope can stop a machine at the moment of danger).

"Those are just examples," Miss Bristoe said. "What they mean is that in the year 2100 people—not only here, but everywhere—will live healthier, longer, fuller, happier lives. From one part of our earth to another will be a quick, safe, pleasant journey—and very likely the same will be true for a journey into outer space."

"That will be something," Bill sighed. "A special something—the year 2100!"

"This year—and the next—and the next—they're all special," Miss Bristoe said. "They're your years, Bill. High adventure awaits you in them. No explorer in all history has come to such wonderful frontiers as now confront you."

"You make me sound as important as old Daniel Boone or Davy Crockett or Kit Carson," Bill chuckled.

"I think you're more important," Miss Bristoe said quietly.

Miss Bristoe pushed back her hair with an impatient sweep of her hand, a gesture Bill had come to understand. The gesture meant that Miss Bristoe believed what she said and if you argued for ten years, you weren't going to change her.

So Bill saved his breath.

# INDEX

PRINTED IN U.S.A.